Jasper Wilson

A letter, commercial and political, addressed to the Rt.
Honble. William Pitt

In which the real Interests of Britain, in the present Crisis, are considered

Jasper Wilson

A letter, commercial and political, addressed to the Rt. Honble. William Pitt
In which the real Interests of Britain, in the present Crisis, are considered

ISBN/EAN: 9783337076146

Printed in Europe, USA, Canada, Australia, Japan

Cover: Foto ©ninafisch / pixelio.de

More available books at **www.hansebooks.com**

PREFACE.

THE following Letter was originally written, as well as printed, in fo hafty a manner, that fome inaccuracies of compofition efcaped notice, as well as feveral errors of the prefs—it was perceived too, on a farther review, that fome illuftrations and additions to particular paffages were wanted, and a fhort, but general fummary of the whole.——Such corrections and enlargements have accordingly been made; a Poftfcript has been added, exemplifying, in fome of the more material points, the application of events fubfequent to the original publication of the Letter, to the reprefentations and reafonings it contains; and the whole, it is hoped, will now be found lefs unworthy of the favourable reception which the firft edition has met with.

LETTER, &c.

SIR,

An inquiry into the caufes of the general calamities which affect the commercial and manufacturing interefts, and the connexion which thefe may have with the meafures of government, feems properly addreffed to you as the Minifter of the Crown, and the Leader of the Houfe of Commons.

A concurrence of fortune and talents has raifed you to a degree of confequence in the public eye which no other individual of the age has attained, and your friends having afcribed to you much of our late unexampled profperity, your enemies will doubtlefs impute to you our prefent unparalleled diftrefs. Party zeal may blind the one and the other; but the fubject of the prefent inquiry muft in every point of view prefs with peculiar force on your mind.

The writer of this was one of the warmeft of your admirers. The progrefs of time and of events has cooled his enthufiafm refpecting you, but has not, as is often the cafe, turned it into hoftility. Neither difpofed to offend or flatter, he would deliver his fentiments with the deference due to

B   your

your extraordinary talents, but with the earneſtneſs and ſolemnity ſuited to the preſent criſis of human affairs.

That the calamities which affect our commerce and manufactures are great beyond example, it is unneceſſary to prove. The unprecedented and alarming meaſures which are reſorted to in parliament to prevent the univerſal wreck of credit, put this beyond a doubt.—It does not however ſeem to be generally obſerved that theſe calamities are not peculiar to Britain. Bankruptcies have ſpread and are ſpreading every where over the continent of Europe, through France, Holland, Germany, Poland, Ruſſia, Italy, and Spain, and every where private as well as public credit is impaired or deſtroyed. If the injury to commerce and manufactures be more felt in Britain than elſewhere, it is becauſe we have had more commerce and manufactures to be injured. And this reaſon, which explains why Britain ſuffers apparently more than the other kingdoms of Europe, will alſo explain why the different towns and counties of Britain ſuffer at preſent exactly in proportion to their former commercial proſperity. In one reſpect England differs at this juncture from moſt of the other European nations—our public credit is yet tolerably ſound—Whilſt the governments of Ruſſia, Auſtria, Poland, France, and Spain, are either bankrupt, or on the verge of bankruptcy, and have had recourſe to practices that differ little from open rapine.

I ſtate theſe facts on authorities to ſome of which I ſhall allude as I go on, but I believe that you will admit them at once as unqueſtionable.

To ſeek for the origin of ſuch general calamities within the precincts of a ſingle kingdom, is to labour to no purpoſe. They are to be traced, as it appears, to the prevalence and extenſion of the war-ſyſtem throughout Europe, ſupported as it has been by the univerſal adoption of the funding-ſyſtem. As this idea has not been laid before the public, as perhaps

haps it may not have prefented itfelf fully even to your mind, and as it feems to be of the utmoft importance, I muft beg leave to unfold it at fome length, and to fhew its application to our own diftreffes.

Speculative men, Sir, in the retirement of their clofets, have delighted to contemplate the progrefs of knowledge, and to fhew its happy effects on the condition of our fpecies. The truth feems to be, as was afferted by Lord Bacon, that " knowledge is power," or, to fpeak more popularly, that power is increafed in proportion to knowledge. But the effects of power on human happinefs depend on the wifdom and benevolence by which it is directed; and where thefe are not found in a correfponding degree, an increafe of power muft often add to the miferies of the human race. Without however difputing the happy influences of the progrefs of knowledge on the whole, it may be doubted whether thefe have extended in any confiderable degree to the general political fyftem; and it may be clearly fhewn, that its effects on the intercourfe of nations with each other, have been hitherto in many refpects injurious.

Among favages the means of intercourfe are reftricted to tribes who are neighbours, and hoftilities are confined in the fame manner. As knowledge increafes, thefe means are multiplied and extended, and nations not in immediate vicinity learn to mingle in each other's affairs. This is abundantly proved by the hiftory of European nations, among whom treaties offenfive and defenfive have, with their communication with each other, been conftantly increafing for the two laft centuries; and wars, without becoming lefs frequent, have become far more general, bloody, and expenfive. The balance of power, a notion fpringing up among ftatefmen towards the end of the 15th century, has been a principal caufe both of the frequency and the extenfivenefs of modern wars; the religious diftinctions which divided Europe

after

after the period of the reformation, have also been the cause
or the pretext of frequent hostilities; and the supposed dignity of crowns, an expression the more dangerous from the
obscurity of its meaning, has been constantly enumerated
among the reasons which justified the inhabitants of different countries in rushing to the destruction of each other.

Wars thus originating in causes peculiar to a semi-bar-
barous state of society, have been extended in other respects
by the progress of knowledge and its effects on the arts.
To this we are to attribute many of the improvements in the
science of destruction, and in the science of finance : to this
especially we are to attribute the *funding-system*, which at
once multiplied the means of warfare twenty-fold, and which,
after anticipating and exhausting the public revenue in almost
every nation of Europe, seems at length to approach the
point so clearly foretold, when it must produce a system of
general peace, or of universal desolation.

The Italian Republics, according to Dr. Smith, first
invented funding—from them it passed to Spain, and from
the Spaniards to the rest of the European nations. The
practice of funding commenced in England with our national
debt during the war which terminated in the peace at Rys-
wick in the year 1697, and it has been the means by which
this debt has accumulated to its present enormous amount.
The system itself is precisely the same as to the community,
that mortgaging the revenue of an estate to raise a present
sum of money, is to the individual. The income mortgaged by the individual arises perhaps from land, that of the
state from one or more taxes ; and both in the one case and
in the other, this mortgage is for the payment of the interest
of the sum borrowed. The individual generally engages to
repay the principal when demanded ; the state never does this,
but while the interest is regularly discharged, and the country is tolerably prosperous, the security given by the state
being

being transferable, finds a ready market, and thus the ab-
forption of the capital, as far as refpects the creditor of the
ftate, is in a great meafure remedied.

The convenience of the funding-fyftem to thofe who adminifter the governments of Europe is obvious.—It enables
them on the commencement of wars to multiply their refources for the moment, perhaps twenty-fold. Previous to
this invention, a tax raifing five hundred thoufand pounds
annually, would have ftrengthened the hands of government
by this fum only ; but under the funding-fyftem, the tax
being mortgaged for ever for as much money as it will pay
the annual intereft of, brings into the treafury the capital
fum at once, that is, ten or perhaps twelve millions. It is
true this fpendthrift expenditure muft bring a day of reckon-
ing—But what then ? Thofe who adminifter the public revenue are not owners of the eftate, but in general, tenants at
will, or at moft, have a life intereft in it only. The practice of mortgaging the public revenue during wars prevents
the people from feeling the immediate preffure of the expence,
by transferring it in a great meafure to pofterity. Minifters
look to the prefent moment, and delight in expedients that
may delay the evil day.—When it comes, it does not in all
probability fall on thofe with whom the mifchief originated.
They are no longer in power; they are perhaps in their
graves, and removed from the complaints and wrongs of their
injured country.

It is however but candid to acknowledge, that we have
feen you acting on a fuperior fyftem; incurring the odium
of propofing new taxes, to difcharge the intereft of debts con-
tracted in fupport of meafures which you had uniformly oppofed, and teaching almoft an exhaufted people to bear ftill
heavier burthens, rather than facrifice their future good, or
violate the eternal obligations of juftice!—Then was your
day of triumph.

Half

Half informed men have sometimes contended that the national debt is a national good. To enter at large into their arguments is foreign to my purpose, since this position depends on sophisms that have been often detected. It may indeed be admitted that some accidental advantages have arisen from the transferable and marketable nature of the securities given to the public creditors: In times of commercial prosperity these have promoted circulation, and acted in some degree like a quantity of well-secured paper money: But this effect, besides that it is contingent and uncertain, in no respect compensates for the evils arising from the pressure of taxes, the increased rate of wages, and the withdrawing of an immense **capital from productive** to unproductive labour *.

Without embarrassing ourselves with complicated ideas, it may be at once asserted, that a nation which goes on borrowing and mortgaging without redeeming its funds, must at length, like an individual, become bankrupt, and that the ruin this produces will correspond to the magnitude of the bankruptcy. This has been all along clearly foreseen by those who have examined the subject; but the predictions of some enlightened men, as to the sum of debt under which the nation must become bankrupt, having turned out fallacious, ignorant persons have supposed that the principle, on which these predictions were founded, was in itself false. But admitting that Mr. Hume † predicted that a debt of a hundred millions would bring on a national bankruptcy, he erred in his calculation only from not foreseeing the influence of the progress of knowledge on the useful arts, and the increased sources of re-

---

* See the Wealth of Nations.

† It does not appear that Mr. Hume was the author of this prediction, which has been generally ascribed to him.—It is however evident from his Essay on Public Credit, that he did not foresee the great amount to which the debt might be carried—a circumstance easily explained.

venue which would thus be opened. The furprifing advances of chemiftry, and the effects of its application to manufactures; the wonderful combinations of chemiftry and mechanics, for the reduction of labour—thefe are the happy means by which bankruptcy has been hitherto averted. The fecurity of property and the fpirit of liberty diffufed through the nation, have called forth the talents of our people. Britain has grown profperous in fpite of the wretched politics of her rulers. The genius of Watt, Wedgewood, and Arkwright, has counteracted the expenfe and folly of the American war.

Are we to go on for ever in this extraordinary career * ? It is impoffible! the fources through which we have been enabled to fuftain our enormous burthens are in a great meafure dried up, our burthens themfelves are increafing, and the whole fabric of our profperity totters to its bafe!

Our profperity depends on commerce; commerce requires peace, and all the world is at war—this is the fhort and the melancholy hiftory of our fituation. The fhock is felt in England more than elfewhere, becaufe, as was faid before, England is more commercial than any other nation, but it pervades more or lefs the continent of Europe, from St. Peterfburgh to Leghorn: the hiftory of commerce records no calamity fo fevere and fo extenfive. Of the houfes that remain folvent, it is known, that the greater part are ftruggling with difficulties; that thefe are hourly increafing; and that diftruft and difmay prevail univerfally. In Britain, as I fhall have occafion to fhew, our mercantile diftreffes are aggravated by the imprudent confidence, arifing out of extra-

* I might have anfwered this queftion in the words of Mr. Chalmers, in his "Comparative Eftimate," where he very juftly decides, that we can go on incurring debt, and frefh taxes, only while commerce and manufactures increafe in a correfponding degree. This mafterly work will throw much light on our prefent fituation; Lord Hawkefbury will do well to perufe it once more.

ordinary

ordinary profperity, which produced a very general over-trading of capital, and in fome places a fpirit of very unjuftifiable fpeculation; but on the continent, where bankruptcy and diftrefs began firft, the imprudence of the mercantile fyftem feems to have had little fhare in the failures, which may be traced almoft entirely to the war politics of the ruling powers, and the dreadful practices by which thefe have been fupported.

Whoever examines the hiftory of the military eftablifhments of the different European nations, will find that they have been for more than two hundred years almoft every where regularly increafing. The means of fupporting this increafe may have been found, in part, in the gradual augmentation of opulence and population, which perhaps has taken place pretty generally, in fpite of the burthen of thefe eftablifhments.—But the very great and fudden increafe of the armies brought into the field in the latter end of the laft, and the beginning of the prefent century, is clearly to be attributed to the funding-fyftem, which about this time became almoft univerfal. From this period the ftanding forces of Europe during peace have been gradually and regularly augmenting as before, and each fucceffive war has produced more numerous and better appointed armies than that which preceded.—The forces employed, the expenfe incurred, and the deftruction produced in the war which terminated in the peace of 1763, far exceeded whatever was before known in the annals of hiftory. Satiated and exhaufted with flaughter, the nations of Chriftendom funk down into a fhort-lived repofe. This was foon difturbed by the emprefs of Ruffia, whofe reign has involved her fubjects in perpetual diftreffes, her neighbours in conftant alarms, and has filled the eaftern parts of Europe with repeated carnage *. In the weft, the

torch

* This fingular woman affects to be a patronefs of learning, and is not deftitute of what are called the princely virtues. She has had a kind of humour

the torch of war was rekindled by England, an a conflict with her own colonies aided by France, more fruitless, fierce, and bloody, than the war of 1756, dissevered her empire, added a hundred millions to her debt, and six millions annually to her standing taxes [*].

During these operations in the east and west, the centre of Europe was agitated by the restless and pragmatic temper of the Emperor Joseph. This unwise and unfortunate, but not ill-intentioned prince, was happily controlled by the talents of the great Frederick, who for the last twenty years of his life cultivated the arts of peace, and on several occasions stifled the flames of a general war. The example of the King of Prussia, however, and the mutual jealousy of the continental powers, wonderfully increased the armies of the continent, and during his reign the peace establishment of Germany, a country containing less than eighteen millions of people, rose to five or six hundred thousand soldiers! By his superior policy the King of Prussia indeed contrived to render his army comparatively little burthensome to his subjects, and died with his treasury full [†]. But Austria and all the inferior powers of Germany have been long very poor. The wants of Joseph

---

mour of sending her picture in gold snuff-boxes to literary men in different parts of Europe. Praise has been openly bestowed on her by Zimmermann, and indeed insinuated by Robertson. Impartial history will record the steps by which the *wife of Peter III. ascended her throne*; it will tell of 30,000 Turks massacred in cold blood at Ismael; it will describe the first and the second division of Poland; and the annalist of better times may record this " august patroness of letters" as the scourge of the human race.

[*] By the first of these wars we conquered America, by the second we lost it, and thus a balance was struck; but two hundred millions of debt was incurred, and five hundred thousand lives sacrificed!—" What hath pride " profited us? Or what good have riches with our vaunting brought us? All " these things are passed away like a shadow, and as a post that hasted by."

Wisdom of Solomon.

[†] His successor, it is generally understood, has nearly, if not entirely, dissipated his treasures.

C

were great, thofe of Leopold greater, and thofe of the prefent Emperor are extreme—Ruffia is abfolutely bankrupt, and the whole body of the peafantry reduced to the moft wretched poverty. Spain languifhes under an immenfe load of debt; and the fame may be faid of Holland, Portugal, and, as I am informed, of the northern powers—The fituation of France needs not to be defcribed.

A philofophical mind will difcover in every page of hiftory, and will lament, while it excufes, the fatal ignorance of thofe by whom nations have been governed. General invectives againft fuch characters are however unjuft; the Rulers of the world ought to be approached with mingled refpect and pity. Supreme power to its proper exercife requires perfect wifdom, and monarchs as well as minifters are weak, fallible and ignorant, like ourfelves. Hence it is that we find them in all ages wafting the little hoards of property acquired by private induftry, in projects of foolifh vanity, or of ftill more foolifh ambition. And hence it is that, during the laft century, we have feen them convert even the acquifitions of fcience and of the arts, rifing unprotected in fociety, to the fame fatal purpofes; carrying the fury of war by this means into the moft remote feas and regions, and exhaufting not only the patrimony of a fingle generation in their rafh and ruinous projects, but that of new generations of men for a long fucceffion of years.

In the order of Providence, great evils bring their own remedies, and the funding-fyftem, by exhaufting the means of fupporting war, has a tendency to produce univerfal peace. But it is melancholy to reflect on the national bankruptcies, which it muft probably render general in the firft inftance. Their effects will vary as the people are more or lefs commercial, more or lefs enlightened. They may for a time rivet the chains of defpotifm, as in Ruffia; or raife a bloody anarchy on the ruins of monarchy, as in France. A fyftem of general peace, adopted fpeedily, may avert a great part of the calamities which hang over Europe; but,

while

while paffion and prejudice fo generally predominate, this, alas! is rather an object of our wifhes than our hopes.

It ought however to make a deep impreffion on thofe who are entrufted with the happinefs of nations, that the direct caufe of all the troubles in France was the lavifh expenditure of its old government fupported by the funding-fyftem. The war of 1756, and that undertaken for the Americans, brought this fyftem to its crifis; the revenue was more than anticipated by the intereft of debts and the expenfe of the government; frefh taxes could not be collected; the people called loudly for a redrefs of grievances: the court gave way; popular affemblies were fummoned, and followed each other in rapid fucceffion; the current of opinion fet ftronger every day againft every thing eftablifhed: the populace found their ftrength; numbers, inftead of wifdom, began to govern; the practice of change begot a habit of changing, and property and principles were fwept away *.

Happily

---

* It is the fate of defpotic governments to be placed in general in the hands of fools; and where folly commands, it is ignorance alone that can be obedient. Nothing ever was fo palpably abfurd as the principles on which France mingled in the American war. She wifhed to weaken England, and threw her force into the American fcale. We had got into a conteft which muft have been long, expenfive, and finally unfuccefsful, even had the abfolute conqueft of the colonies crowned the firft years of the war. We were likely, from our pride and prejudices, to perfevere to the uttermoft, and national bankruptcy could only have arrefted our career. France might have looked on in fecurity, taken the opportunity of the calm to have arranged her finances, reformed her abufes, and ftrengthened herfelf by the arts of peace. She might have rifen on our ruins, the emprefs of the fea, and the arbitrefs of Europe.—She openly interfered—the difeafe which feemed lingering and mortal, fuddenly became violent: a crifis took place; we threw off the colonies, acknowledged their independence, and, reaffuming the arts of peace, became in a few years more profperous than before. In the mean time France had received a mortal wound; *to prevent the war from becoming unpopular under the exifting burthens*, fhe had carried it on without new taxes,

C 2

by

Happily for England, by great and virtuous exertions, she escaped in the year 1783 the bankruptcy which France incurred. The effects of continued peace on a nation such as ours are beyond calculation. National confidence and credit being restored, our manufactures spread over the continents of the old and the new world, and our revenue rose on *the basis of circulation* to its late unexampled height. A paper currency of promissory notes and of bills of exchange was a necessary consequence, and this, which ought to have represented specie or merchandise only, became in a season of singular prosperity the representation of almost every kind of property fixed and unfixed.

In the mean time affairs on the continent assumed a hostile aspect. The allied powers began to arm; France

by borrowing only. When peace came, this new debt was to be provided for—the people were poor, discontented, and, what was worst of all, they were in some degree enlightened—the rest is known.

The policy of the powers which are combined against France is of the same weak and foolish kind. The folly and the crimes of France rendered a civil war inevitable, and Europe might have looked on in safety and peace. This mighty people, weakened by intestine divisions, would have been no longer formidable; and the process of their experiments on government, if left to itself, would have been fruitful of lessons of the most important kind. The neighbouring monarchs met at Pillnitz, and agreed to invade France the first *convenient opportunity*. The treaty was discovered; it gave victory to the republicans without a contest; a civil war was prevented; and the banner of Jacobinism reigned triumphant. The allied powers have carried their treaty into effect; but being burthened with debt already, and the state of the public mind *requiring to be particularly consulted at present*, they are, like France of old, carrying it on by borrowing without laying on taxes, leaving this for the season of peace. The Emperor I am told gives nine per cent. for money, to prevent the imposition of taxes; and yet it is said that the unreasonable people of Vienna are not satisfied.

So far the policy of the powers now allied against France, and that of France herself in the American war, are precisely similar—How far the effects may correspond is in the womb of time.

armed

armed also. Armaments, in countries comparatively speaking little commercial, required specie. It probably flowed freely from England, for a paper circulation supplied its place. These armaments rendered the people, as well as the governments, poor, by diminishing and oppressing productive labour, absorbing the wealth that should have been employed in private industry, and obstructing commercial intercourse. Hence our customers did not purchase, or did not pay for our manufactures, and they began to remain on our hands.

Certain circumstances however prevented for a time our feeling the full effect of the war politics on the continent. In the first place we were at peace, and had declared for a peace-system, while the rest of Europe was agitated, and under arms. Hence our funds became a favourite object of purchase for those monied men on the continent who wished to secure their property; immense sums, it is said, flowed in from France and the Low Countries, and the prices of stock rose for a time, with the decline of our export of manufactures, and the efflux, as it should seem, of the precious metals.

Another circumstance operated in our favour. The war on the continent increased the demand for particular manufactures, from Germany, and more especially from France—Birmingham felt this, so did Yorkshire. Burning for combat, the *Sans Culottes* rushed into the field—and Arms! Arms and clothing! was echoed from Picardy to Provence. These demands could only be supplied by England. France had ruined her credit by her second revolution: she must come to market with specie; and her gold and silver might have rested with us.—Our true policy was clear.

By this time however the sympathies of the different parties in England were excited to such a degree by the state of things on the continent, that the dictates of sound reason
could

could no longer be heard; and the wickedness of the ruling party in France having perpetrated one deliberate and dreadful murder, calculated to awake the horror of men in an extraordinary degree, the original friends of the revolution became mute; the once sacred name of Liberty itself became offensive; the alarmists rose suddenly in numbers and force; clamours and indignation sprung up in every quarter; and, amidst a wild uproar of false terrors and of virtuous sympathy, the nation was plunged headlong into this dreadful war!

One powerful voice indeed was heard above the storm, but the accents of reason and truth sounded like treason to an irritated people, and our rulers joined in the general outcry; the friends of peace incurred the foulest calumnies of the day, but secured to themselves the purest admiration, when passion and prejudice shall be no more.

War came; and fast on its heels a dreadful train of evils—bankruptcy followed bankruptcy in rapid succession, our resources seemed to vanish, distrust and terror seised the mercantile world, and the Bank of England itself partook, as it is reported, of the general alarm. In the mean time you are said to have declared in your place, that these evils had no connexion with the war, and Mr. Dundas assured us that they arose from our extraordinary prosperity. Similar language is made use of by the partizans of administration every where, and it is fit that this dreadful error should be publicly unveiled.

In a season of general peace and great prosperity, private as well as public credit had arisen to an extraordinary height, and, from causes very obvious, but which it would be tedious to enumerate, paper-money became in a great measure the medium of circulation. This paper consisted of two kinds; of bills of exchange payable at different dates, and generally discountable; and of promissory notes, issued by the Bank of England and private Banking-houses, payable in specie on demand. The credit of each of these depended on their representing a property real and secure. The promissory notes were indeed supposed to represent specie at all times ready on demand, but in reality rested for their credit on the basis of some fixed property within the kingdom, and frequently on landed estates. The bills of exchange depended for their circulation on the joint credit of the drawer and the acceptor, and represented in a great measure property out of the kingdom ; perhaps on the seas, in the West Indies, on the coast of Africa, in America, or on the continent of Europe *. By means of this medium a vast quantity of fixed property was brought, as it were, into a state of activity ; the paper money in circulation, every kind included, amounting, as I have been told, to a sum that seems almost incredible †! The effects of a war on a paper medium, such as I have described, may be easily imagined.—It must diminish the security of all property on the seas, in our islands, on the coast of Africa, &c. and of course destroy or impair the credit of all bills of exchange running on the validity of such property. If the property itself during a war would not easily find a purchaser, neither would a bill resting on that property. The property itself however might still be saleable, though at a diminished value ; but this would not be the case with a bill of exchange, which, if it does not pass for the sum it is drawn for, will pass for nothing, and is thrown out of circulation. The manner in which this distressed our West-India houses is well known. The degree of hazard of our islands was perhaps over-rated, a circumstance arising from the peculiar nature of the war,

---

* This subject is very elegantly and fully explained in a pamphlet intitled " Thoughts on the Causes of the present Failures," published by Johnson.

† Two hundred millions.

and

and the fears under which we laboured, and ftill labour, of the defperate methods to which the French may have recourfe. Previous to the war in England, bankruptcies had begun on the continent, and the fecurity of bills of foreign exchange was every day impaired. The invafion of Holland by Dumourier, one of the firft confequences of the war, was a blow aimed at the credit of all Europe ; our houfes concerned in Dutch and other foreign exchanges found their fecurity particularly fhaken ; many of them are fuppofed to have tottered, and feveral fell. A fimilar effect took place in various parts of the continent, and the action and reaction of ruin fpread far and wide. The invafion and partition of Poland contributed much to this general calamity. The Bank of Warfaw, the depofit of all the furplus wealth of the landed intereft of Poland, was oppreffed and deftroyed by the royal plunderers ; it failed, as it is faid, for ten millions fterling, and brought down with it various houfes throughout Europe, particularly in Peterfburg, Hamburg, and Amfterdam *.

The war deprived our manufactures of the French market, of all others the moft extenfive, and, as it had been conducted for a twelvemonth paft, by far the moft fafe and lucrative. The general wreck of credit among our allies on the continent deprived us in a great meafure of the markets there. Orders did not arrive, or, if they did arrive, could not be executed ; the fecurity of the correfpondent was doubted, or the channel of payment fhut up. It was foon therefore found, that our manufactures for the foreign markets had not fuftained a temporary check, fuch as arifes from overtrading every fixth or feventh year of peace, but an abfolute ftagnation ; the bills and paper running on the fecurity of the capital vefted in machinery (an enormous and lately moft

---

* Fifteen houfes in Peterfburg, concerned in the trade to China, failed together.

productive

productive property) were of courfe fhaken in their credit, and in the courfe of a few weeks, if a profpect of peace does not open, will be of all others the moft infecure. If it were proper on fuch an occafion to bring forward names, each of thefe affertions might be fupported and illuftrated by abundant proofs.

The general refult of thefe particulars is—That whereas, before the war, bills were difcountable, and of courfe entered into circulation from every part of the world, at perhaps eighteen months date, and fometimes at even longer, diftruft and bankruptcy have, for the prefent, rendered three-fourths of the whole wafte paper; and thofe of the very firft credit are in general negotiable at two months date only. The immenfe chafm that this muft make in circulation may be eafily imagined.

This general diftrefs in the commercial and manufacturing interefts muft, of courfe, occafion a great preffure on the monied men. What is their fituation? Their property is generally vefted in public fecurities; thefe muft be fold out to meet the exigence, at a lofs of from 20 to 25 per cent. Public fecurities have already funk in value in confequence of the war, to the amount of nearly fifty millions fterling, a fum almoft equal to the whole of our national debt at the commencement of the war of 1755!

Land has not efcaped deterioration; but, for obvious reafons, except in the immediate vicinity of towns, it has fuffered lefs than any other property; and of courfe the fecurity of promiffory notes iffued by country banking-houfes, as far as they depended on landed eftates, is, or ought to be, lefs affected than any other. In the general panic, indeed, runs have been made on almoft every houfe of this kind; a few have failed from infufficient ftability, and many have flopped payment for want of fpecie. But in general thofe who have

D
fhewn

shewn a sufficient foundation of real property, have been supported by public confidence, and, in the absolute scarcity of gold and silver, their notes have returned into circulation. In situations where this has happened, the distress is far less than where no circulation of such promissory notes had taken place. It seems the more necessary to state these facts, because, in both houses of parliament, some respectable individuals seem disposed to impute our present distresses in a great measure to the increase of banking-houses issuing promissory notes*.

It may be observed, that circulating notes of this kind, each representing a guinea, have long been the universal medium throughout Scotland, where the commercial distress, though great, is much less than in England; not more than one banking-house there having as yet failed. Five pound notes of the same kind are in common circulation through several of the northern counties, and, in the moment of general panic, were much exclaimed against. But the alarm is subsiding, and confidence returns †. The truth will soon appear to be, that a well-secured and well-regulated—medium of this kind is at this instant of essential service where it circulates; and it is very probable that it will be resorted to in situations where it has not yet been adopted. In Lancashire, where the distress both in the commercial and manufacturing interests is perhaps greater than in any part of the kingdom, promissory notes were never issued by any of the banking-houses; and to this, I will venture to say, the universal stagnation there is in some degree to be attributed. The necessity of resorting to a paper-money generally, which cannot be immediately commuted into specie, would indeed be a

* The Duke of Norfolk is one who has fallen into this mistake.

† See the proceedings at Newcastle, Whitehaven, &c.

proof

proof of extraordinary diſtreſs, but it may one day come. There is a ſituation that a good citizen muſt brood over in ſilence, but which the rapid career of our adverſity does not admit to be long abſent from his thoughts, in which it may be the only national remedy againſt general ruin and confuſion.

Though the banking-houſes which circulate promiſſory notes have not contributed in any conſiderable degree to our preſent diſtreſs, it muſt be admitted that it has been aggravated by the imprudence of individuals in over-trading their capitals, and reſorting in ſeveral inſtances to the ſyſtem of drawing and redrawing for ſupporting their credit *. This however is a diſeaſe which has a conſtant tendency to ariſe in ſeaſons of great proſperity, and which, though it operate ſeverely on particular places, cannot be conſidered as entering largely into our national diſtreſs:—not having been without its effect, it gives I preſume a colour to the aſſertion of Mr. Dundas; but will even Mr. Dundas ſay, that the imprudence of a few individuals has deſtroyed the whole market of our manufactures, or lowered the funds fifty millions?

To this general repreſentation an objection will perhaps occur, that it explains things too clearly; that events can ſeldom be traced in this regular way; and that politics do not afford any thing ſo nearly approaching to demonſtration. The reply to this is eaſy—Politics have generally for their object the conduct of cabinets; and the uncertainty to which they are liable is chiefly to be imputed to the ignorance and caprice by which cabinets are governed. Hence the difficulty of predicting how they may act ariſes from

* Thoſe who wiſh to ſee this clearly and fully explained, may conſult the Wealth of Nations, laſt edition.

the

the impoffibility of forefeeing, with any certainty, their motives of action. But that part of the political œconomy which unfolds the theory of trade and manufactures, approaches to the nature of fcience, becaufe it has the intercourfe of commercial men for its object, who are conftantly governed by a fenfe of intereft, the moft uniform motive of human conduct. We diftinguifh-ill, if we fuppofe that what refpects commerce is equally uncertain with what refpects politics; the freaks of the mifchievous monkey are indeed wild and capricious, but the actions of the induftrious beaver are uniform and exact. It may alfo be objected to this explanation of the caufes of our diftrefs, that it is founded on principles which apply to former wars as well as to that we are engaged in, while our prefent calamities are altogether fingular and unprecedented. It muft be admitted that our diftreffes are fingular in degree, but they are not fingular in their nature; in the commencement of all our wars, induftry and credit have fuftained a fimilar blow, and it only remains to be fhewn why the prefent fhock is fo peculiarly fevere and tremendous.

That the entrance of war has always injured our commercial profperity, may be proved from the authentic documents in Mr. Chalmers's " Comparative Eftimate;" and thofe who remember the commencement of the laft war, muft alfo recollect the diftrefs which it occafioned. The extraordinary ruin of the prefent moment, compared with that of 1755 or 1775, is to be traced to the change which this nation, as well as the other nations of Europe, has been gradually undergoing, and to the peculiar nature and feat of the exifting warfare. At the breaking out of the war in 1755, the debt of Great Britain amounted to feventy-two millions; and now the debt funded and unfunded is nearly two hundred and fifty millions. We fet out on the prefent occafion occasion under an additional weight of almost two hundred millions!

But let us take the commencement of the last war, a period still fresh in our recollections, and when the disparity of situation was not so great. In the beginning of February, you held out a prospect that the existing revenue was not likely to fall off in consequence of the present hostilities, because in the first year of the last war it was not much affected. You seemed to admit that the *progress* of our commerce and manufactures might indeed be stopped, but you did not apprehend there would be much, if any, diminution of what we already possessed. The melancholy records of the last three months have detected this fatal error, to which perhaps the war itself is in some degree owing, and, painful as is the office, there may yet be some advantage in tracing it to its source. The American war commenced in a gradual manner—Our disputes with the colonists had been of several years continuance, and before hostilities broke out our merchants had foreseen them and provided against them. The provision, it is true, was far from complete; for though in the year immediately preceding the war very unusual remittances were made from America, yet, on the opening of hostilities, a large capital was locked up in that country, by which the trade of London, Bristol, and Liverpool, was considerably injured, and at Glasgow and Whitehaven a very extensive bankruptcy took place. A circumstance however distinguished those times from the present, which is of material importance.—Previous to the war of 1775, our manufacturers were not much in the habit of exporting on their own accounts. They received their orders chiefly from the merchants here, at whose risque the manufactures were shipped; so that though the mercantile houses received a severe blow in the rupture with America, the manufacturing capital

capital was, comparatively speaking, little injured. What contributed a good deal to this, was the prohibition of importation laid by the American Congress the year before the war, at a time when remittances to this country were allowed, and were so considerable. In consequence of this, our manufacturers, with their skill and their capitals unimpaired, began early to explore new markets, and to improve those already known; and from this date commenced that rapid increase of export to the continent of Europe, which saved us from national bankruptcy, and raised us again to our rank among nations. It was soon found that the American market was, comparatively speaking, of little value; and it was found also, that the superiority of our manufactures forced their way into it, notwithstanding the obstructions of the war. They took a circuitous course indeed through Holland; but Yorkshire furnished the greater part of the clothing of the Sans Culottes of America; and though they had set up a republican government, and were rebels, not against Louis XVI. but our own gracious King—no Traitorous Correspondence Bill was moved for by the Attorney General of the day*.

Since the last peace however our manufacturers have almost universally acted as merchants, and shipped their goods on their own account. They have gained possession of

* It was during this period, if my memory does not fail me, that the Duke of Richmond, who has been so loyally employed of late in fortifying the Tower, was accused in the ministerial papers of having surveyed some parts of the coast, for the purpose of directing the French where they might with safety attack us; it was at this time that Mr. Burke openly boasted in the House of Commons, of corresponding with the republican-rebel Franklin, intriguing at Paris to bring all Europe on our heads; it was during the same calamitous period that a young Statesman, since so well known throughout Europe, began his career, by justifying the republicans of America in their resistance, and reprobating, as the height of wickedness and insanity, our design of subjugating them by force.

the

the foreign markets, in part from the superiority of their
skill, but far more from the superiority of their capital,
which has enabled them to give a credit almost every where
from twelve to eighteen months. Hence at the present moment our manufacturing capital (contrary to what happened
in the beginning of the last war) is in a great measure in-
vested in foreign debts. The merchants in the ports of the
kingdom felt the calamities of war soonest; but it is on the
manufacturing body that it will fall with the most unrelenting ruin. What adds to the distress of the moment is, that
the war was not, like the American contest, long foreseen.
We had declared for a peace-system; it was clearly our interest to maintain it; it seemed almost suicide in France to
provoke a quarrel: mercantile men in both kingdoms deprecated a rupture, and, reasoning on the grounds of mutual
interest (the familiar and fundamental principle of plain
and sensible men), they could not believe, long after the
horizon began to darken, that a storm would ensue—
When the clouds burst, they were therefore naked and un-
prepared.

The difference in the situation of our public burthens is
also to be considered in comparing the two periods; we commenced the war with America under a debt of 130 millions;
and we start now with a debt of 250:—our peace establishment, the interest of the debt included, was then ten millions annually; it has now mounted to seventeen millions.

It may however be supposed that our ability to pay these
increased burthens has increased in a proportional degree—
I would not undervalue the resources of my country, and I
believe this to be true; but it is only true while we continue
at peace, and preserve as much as possible the peace of the
world. If indeed our ability to pay taxes were measured by
the state of our exports, it might be justly doubted whether

7   it

it has augmented in the degree that is fuppofed *. But this ability depends in reality on the excefs of our productive labour over our wants; and the facility of collecting taxes, a point very important, depends in a great meafure on the degree of confumption and circulation.—The excefs of our productive labour does not appear in our exports, as fome are apt to fuppofe, for much of it has been employed in the creation of new capital—in the increafe of buildings and machinery—in the improvement of the foil—and in the opening of new roads and canals, of all modes of employing the national capital by far the moft ufeful †. Thefe improvements were going on with a moft happy and accelerated progrefs; our public burthens were beginning to decreafe with the increafe of our power of bearing them; and England advanced rapidly towards that ultimate point of profperity, the poffibility of which was demonftrated by Dr. A. Smith with a mathematical precifion; and its approach predicted by yourfelf in a ftrain of eloquence that gave to truth all the charms

* The average of our exports for the laft ten years does not, it is faid, exceed feventeen millions; which is not more than three millions greater than the amount they averaged in an equal number of years before the American war. The documents on this fubject however are not fufficient for accurate ftatement.

See *Mr. Chalmers's Comparative Eftimate.*

† In Lancafhire alone, one million of the profits of manufactures and commerce is about to be invefted in canals now forming there, if the diftreffes of the times permit the fubfcriptions to be paid; and fuch of the labouring manufacturers as are employed at all, are now chiefly employed in forming thefe canals. The happy effects of fuch an application of capital in a fingle county, and fuch a county as Lancafhire, no one can eftimate, but they depend almoft entirely on peace. The war has already funk the value of fhares in this property greatly, and it has diminifhed the carriage on the canals already made, more than one half. On this fubject authentic information may be obtained from the Duke of Bridgewater. I fpeak on the authority of a well-informed correfpondent.

of

of fiction, and unfolded to an admiring nation, a prospect of real happiness, supposed only to exist in the poet's dream * ! You knew, however, and you acknowledged, that the continuation of peace was neceffary to enfure the bleffings you foretold—happy had it been for the nation, if you had feen that it was indifpenfable to the duration of thofe we already enjoyed !

It has been imagined by many, that the prefent war ought to be light in comparifon of the laft, becaufe then we fought alone, and now all the world is in alliance with us. Mr. Dundas in the Houfe of Commons boafted of this; and declared the intention of miniftry was to bring, if poffible, every nation of Europe upon France. It is, I prefume, in confequence of the operations of this policy, before it was avowed, that Spain and Pruffia are now in arms, and that Portugal, Turkey, and the Northern Powers, are openly folicited to join the general confederacy—Weak and miferable policy ! Better far had it been for Britain to have fought France fingly, if her power had been twice as great, while the reft of Europe looked on, than to ftir up and mingle in this general crufade of folly and ruin. I fpeak not in the language of a moralift, but of a politician; and of this affertion I challenge the moft rigid examination.—What fupported us during the American war ? the export of our manufactures to countries that could purchafe them, becaufe they enjoyed the bleffings of peace. But who is there now to buy our manufactures ? where is peace now to be found ? The nations of Europe are in arms from the White Sea to the Pillars of Hercules, and in the courfe of the fummer there will be upwards of two millions of men in the field. Ancient or modern hiftory ftates

* See Mr. Pitt's fpeech, 17th Feb. 1792, on his motion for taking off a part of our taxes.

E

nothing

nothing equal to the expense or the extent of this armament, undertaken when the funds of all the belligerent powers are anticipated and exhausted, and national credit is everywhere (England I hope excepted) about to explode. If the whole population of Europe be a hundred and twenty millions, it will contain twenty-five or thirty millions of men fit for labour, or what are called fighting men. Of this number there is a 12th or 15th part taken from a productive labour to that which produces nothing; or, what illustrates the point more clearly, brought into the same situation with respect to the public as if the whole became paralytic in a day, and yet required not only the same subsistence as when capable of labour, but one much more expensive. But as the men called into the field are in the flower of life, the productive labour diminished will be more than in proportion to their numbers; and as they are to combat far from home, the expense of their maintenance while soldiers will double and treble what mere cessation from labour would have produced. The stock of productive labour must however not only be subject to all former burthens, but oppressed with the maintenance of the labourers taken from it and turned into soldiers, and thus the loss will be more than doubled. It is possible that in some parts of Europe famine may arise, but this is not likely to be a general or an immediate effect. Subsistence is such an evident want, and such an irrestible call, that the ground will always be cultivated in the first instance. The labourers taken from agriculture for the field, will have their places supplied by others deprived of their usual labour in manufactures, which the war has injured or ruined; and poverty, by teaching men less expensive habits both of diet and clothing, will protract the hour of absolute want. It is in the seat of war only that famine may be considered as inevitable; it is there also that disease may soon be expected; contagion will scatter her poison, and destroy more than the sword. The

elasticity

elasticity of human exertions cannot be exactly calculated; and it would be rash to predict, how, or to what extent these may operate under burthens so heavy and so general. It seems however unavoidable that, during the continuance of the war, these burthens must every where increase. If the support of life becomes even difficult, the collection of revenue will become impossible: from the shrivelled muscles and dried bones of their starving peasantry, the conquerors of Poland and the invaders of France will not be able to extract **the support** of their senseless ambition and foolish waste.

It is evident that this general poverty must operate peculiarly, and every day more heavily, on Britain. Since the last war this country has become the store-house of the nations of Europe, and has furnished almost the whole stock of the superfluities they have been enabled to buy. We see clearly that it is the consumption of these superfluities which the war must first destroy; experience has rendered this truth incontestible. Those who live by the manufacture of these superfluities, must therefore be the first and greatest sufferers in every part of Europe, and unfortunately the greater part of this description of men live here. Here then the ruin must be most severely felt, and our sufferings will be the greater and the harder to bear, because they will be in the **exact** proportion of our former *prosperity*. It is very clear then, that had we even ourselves continued at peace, while the other belligerent powers were at war, we should have suffered much from the progress of universal poverty.— There are however advantages attending such a situation, which, with prudent management, might have born us through the difficulties. We should have supplied the clothing of the various armies in the field; we should have enjoyed a monopoly of the sale of arms, artillery, and **the** other means of destruction; we should have become the universal carriers of provisions and warlike stores; we should

E 2

have

have been enabled to convey our own manufactures in safety wherever any sale for them remained ; and we should have been saved the enormous and destructive expense of arming and protecting our extended commerce in the different quarters of the globe. Our possessions in the east and in the west would have remained secure, and the credit of our paper circulation continued unimpaired. While the storm raged on the land, England might have declared the ocean inviolable ; and if the warring powers had disturbed it, she might have reared her head above the waves, extended her immortal trident, and bid the tempest be still *. Holding in her possession a great part of the clothing, the arms, and the stores of the powers at war, and being at the same time the undisputed mistress of the sea, and the great channel of intercourse between nations—when the strength and fury of conflicting passions were sated with blood, or subdued with slaughter, she might have denounced her vengeance on the aggressors, have offered her succours to the oppressed, and dictated the term of universal peace.—Such our situation might have been—nay, must have been, had we not become parties in the general strife. What is our situation now ? We are involved ourselves in the quarrel ; there is no nation of Europe left to mediate between the conflicting powers ; and if England does not again assume the office of umpire, nothing but the extermination of the French , or the downfall of the governments of Germany, seems capable of satisfying the enraged parties, or restoring the peace of the world. But it may be said, it is better for us to fight France now with all the world with us, than to fight her hereafter alone. Why should we fight her at all ?—it is not our interest. But it

* Maturate fugam, regique hæc dicite vestro:
Non illi imperium pelagi, saevumque tridentem ;
Sed mihi forte datum.——   VIRGIL. Æn. I.

may

may be fuppofed that the ambition of France, when her government is fettled, will compel us to go to war in felf-de-
fence. I do not think this likely, becaufe it cannot be *her*
intereft; but we will allow the fuppofition. If France attack
us, it muft be on the fea, our favourite element, and there
fhe will, I doubt not, find our fuperiority once more.—There
fhe found our fuperiority in the American conteft, though fhe
employed her whole refources on her marine, though fhe
was aided by Spain, Holland and America, and though fhe
attacked us when we were in fome degree exhaufted by three
expenfive and bloody campaigns.

If France and England combat alone, it muft be on the
fea, and deftructive though the conteft muft be, it is not
likely of itfelf either to endanger our conftitution or deftroy
our credit, as fome have weakly fuppofed. Our conftitution
is enthroned in the hearts of Englifhmen, and will never be
deftroyed by foreign force; our credit depends on our commerce, but more efpecially on our manufactures, which we
know by experience can furvive a rupture with France, and
even increafe during its continuance, *provided the reft of
Europe is at peace* *. Unfortunately at prefent all Europe is
not only engaged in war, but in a war of unexampled defpe-
ration and expenfe, at a time when public debts and taxes
have accumulated to an enormous degree in almoft every
one of the belligerent powers; where the governments (that
of our own country always excepted) are univerfally oppreffive, and the people poor and wretched.

---

* I would not however be underftood to confider a war with France, or
with any other country, in any other light under our circumftances, than in
that of a moft ferious calamity. I wifh to point out the peculiarity in the prefent war, that makes it to us particularly deftructive. It is the general ftate of
warfare, and the confequent poverty, that is our bane. In regard to fome of
the powers now under arms, if they are to be at war, it is of little confequence
to us, as to the actual force they can bring forward, whether they fight with
or againft us.

Fifty years ago, Mr. Hume, treating on the effects of public credit, obferved, that it muft either deftroy the nation, or the nation muft deftroy it. " I muft confefs," fays this profound obferver, " when I fee princes and ftates " quarrelling, amidft their debts, funds, and public mort- " gages, it always brings to my mind a match of cudgel- " playing fought in a china fhop *." Since the time this was written, the public debts of the European nations have been more than doubled, taking the whole together, and thofe of France, Britain, and Ruffia, have increafed almoft fourfold. The figure of Mr. Hume may now perhaps be a little altered. The prefent match of cudgel-playing is indeed in a china-fhop, but the walls of the houfe are now become china alfo. If the performers get very warm in the bufinefs, they may therefore not only deftroy the moveables, but bring the houfe itfelf about their ears.

I heard a member in the Houfe of Commons pleading with great eloquence for our plunging into the war with France, and call out—Perifh our commerce, if it muft perifh, but let our conftitution live!—The words were foolifh:— the feparation is no longer poffible. The vital principle of our conftitution—the divifion and diftribution of its powers, may indeed furvive the ruin of commerce; and provided the whole people be enlightened, it may be perpetuated after the wreck of our power. The fpirit of our religion may be preferved after the decay of our riches, and poverty and forrow may even render it more pure. The equal principle of our laws, now contained and exemplified in five hundred volumes in folio, may appear perhaps as beautiful, when the deftruction of property fhall have rendered 499 volumes of ftatutes obfolete, and a fingle volume comprifes all that our poverty demands. But the bleffings of our conftitution, in the eye of thofe who adminifter, or hope to adminifter its

* Effay on Public Credit.

powers,

powers, depend, I conceive, on our opulence, and muſt periſh with the commerce from which that opulence flows. Let thoſe therefore who wiſh for *things as they are*, beware of war: true patriots, who abhor civil convulſions, will cheriſh the arts of peace.

" Periſh our commerce"—fooliſh words! What affords three millions annually to the poor? A million and a half annually to the church? What ſupplies a million to the civil liſt?—Our commerce. What ſupports the expenſe of our immenſe naval and military eſtabliſhments? All our places and penſions?—What but our commerce? Thirteen millions of our taxes depend on circulation and conſumption, and this thoughtleſs ſenator cries out—" Periſh our commerce, let our conſtitution live!" But how then muſt the neceſſary ſplendour, the patronage, and the far more extenſive influence of the crown be ſupported? And if this ſplendour, patronage, and influence are ſwept away—where is our conſtitution? What ſhall maintain the crown againſt a band of factious nobles cajoling the people with the ſound of liberty to cover their ſelfiſh ambition; or what ſhall defend hereditary honours and property of every kind againſt the great maſs of the nation, now become poor, and therefore deſperate; ravenous, perhaps, from their wants, and terrible from the remainder of ſpirit and pride which has deſcended from better times * ?

Our conſtitution and our commerce have grown up together; their connection was not at firſt a neceſſary one perhaps, but events have rendered it ſuch; the peace and the ſafety of England depend on its being preſerved. Our very habits and manners, and the ſtructure of ſociety among us, are founded on this union. I know the evils of our ſituation, but the heavy load of our debts and taxes muſt teach us to ſubmit. Patience, peace, œconomy, and gradual re-

* The author can throw out hints only at preſent; but in favour of the prerogative of the crown, as things are ſituated, he has much to offer.

formation,

formation, are the remedies that wife men would point out; the chance of more dangerous means being reforted to arifes from the folly of one clafs, who deny thefe evils, and by denying aggravate them; and from the folly of another, who pronounce them intolerable, and would liften to the counfels of enthufiafts or knaves. At prefent, never was a nation more fubmiffive, or more loyal; but a wife minifter will not wantonly try our patience or goad us too much.

. " Perifh our commerce !"—-Let the member for Norwich correct his expreffion. We will excufe the inaccuracy of an ardent and eloquent mind; we will even make allowance for the prejudices of education—In the fchool of Mr. Burke, trade and manufactures are words that found meanly: among the Jefuits of St. Omer's, the words themfelves were perhaps unknown. Early education, natural tafte, and peculiar fublimity of imagination, have made, I prefume, the detail and the exactnefs of commerce difgufting to Mr. Burke; and have furnifhed his mind with thofe grand and obfcure ideas, that affociate with the lofty manners of chivalry, and the Gothic gloom of a darker age. Hence, probably (fince time, by extinguifhing ambition, has reftored the original habits of his mind), we are to explain his ftrong preference of the feudal relicks of our conftitution, and his dread of the progrefs of commerce, as leading to innovation and change. I do not wifh to break a lance with the champion of ariftocracy, or with any of his followers; and I would concede in their favour as much as truth will admit. If our fociety were to be caft anew, if the interefts of our country were alone to be confulted, and the means were entirely at our command—much as commerce is to be valued, it would be wifer and better to give it lefs fhare in our profperity, and at all events to render our revenue independent of foreign trade. How far it might be defirable to control its effects on our manners, and on our habits of

thinking,

thinking, is a queftion that I cannot enter on at prefent. Confulting our tafte, and fetting moral confiderations afide, we fhould perhaps be willing to preferve a greater degree of correctnefs and purity of manners, and more of the nice and high-fpirited fenfe of honour, than commerce generally admits. But if we try different characters by the teft of utility, and found this teft on the actual ftate of the nation, the knight of chivalry and his various offspring, compared to the modern manufacturer or the merchant, feem weak and ufelefs things. Even the country gentleman of England, the moft refpectable character of all thofe *lilies of the valley who neither toil nor fpin,* finks in this comparifon. The proprietor of landed property, who lives on the income of his eftates, can in general be confidered only as the conduit that conveys the wealth of one generation to another. He is a neceffary link in fociety indeed, but his place can at all times be eafily fupplied: in this point of view the poor peafant who cultivates his eftate is of more importance than he. How then fhall we eftimate him when compared with a refpectable manufacturer—with the original genius, for inftance, who has found means to convert our clay into porcelain, and lays all Europe under contribution to England by his genius, tafte, and fkill ? Or what rank will he take, when his exertions are put in competition with the power and enterprife of the merchant, whofe fhips vifit the moft remote fhores and nations; to whom the coafts of Afia and America are familiar; who draws his wealth from the wilds of Nootka or Labrador, and who makes the diftant Pacific yield up its ftores ? Even in his more elevated fituation in the houfe of commons, the country gentleman, however eloquent and virtuous (Mr. Wyndham himfelf), muft not be compared, as an object of national confequence, with a character like this.

To the confiderations which I have offered on the im-

F

portance of **commerce and** manufactures, and on the effects
already produced on them by the war, you, Sir, if you were
more in the habit of explaining ministerial conduct, might
perhaps reply—That the war is a war of neceffity —that it is
likely to be fhort and fuccefsful—and that, at all events, the
dignity of the nation (the phrafe ufed in the American war),
or perhaps of the crown (for this is now the more correct
expreffion of Lord Grenville), is concerned in carrying it on.
On each of thefe points I mean to offer a few obfervations.
I will then endeavour to fhew the ftate the nation is likely to
be in, on the recefs of parliament; I will make fome obfervations on the terrible refponfibility that minifters affume,
and **conclude with one or two** remarks addreffed more particularly to yourfelf.

The war was neceffary, as its fupporters fay; and this
neceffity is explained in different ways.—By a few it is
afferted, that the French were determined to quarrel with us,
and that they declared war againft us at a time when it
was unexpected and unprovoked. This language however
is held by very few, and is indeed fo utterly inconfiftent both
with fact and probability, that nothing but ignorance or dif-
ingenuoufnefs can employ it. The French were fighting, or
thought they were fighting, for their national exiftence,
againft a combination of the moft alarming kind—To what
purpofe fhould they add England to the number of their
enemies?—England, whofe power they knew by fatal experience—whofe irrefiftible force on the ocean they had repeat-
edly funk under—and whofe neutrality feemed almoft effen-
tial to their procuring the means of carrying on the war. If
it be afferted that they hoped to excite commotions among us,
peace feemed neceffary to this fcheme; for during peace only
could they carry on the intercourfe which fuch a plan would
require. Idle threats of internal commotions were indeed
thrown out by fome individuals among them; but that thefe

commotions

commotions would be directly promoted by an open war, this, could only be sincerely expected by men who were before insane. It may however be said, that insanity did in reality pervade their councils, or those at least by whom their councils were influenced; and indeed this supposition seems in a great measure founded on truth. But the reply to this is clear: how far soever their insanity might go, it did not extend to a war with England, a calamity not only deprecated by their rulers, but by the whole body of the people. There is not an individual who has been in France since the revolution, who will not confirm this truth*. The manner in which this fierce nation humbled itself to England in negociation, was indeed very remarkable; and though in a moment of wounded pride, the actual declaration of war came from them, yet they soon repented of their conduct, and are now openly renewing their endeavours, one might almost say, their solicitations, for peace†. Peace and war, Mr. Pitt, were in your choice—they are in your choice now; you made your election of the latter—you adhere to it—to the late application of Le Brun, it is said, you have not even vouchsafed an answer.

It might seem, indeed, from the whole of your conduct towards France for a twelvemonth past, that England had a particular interest in the continuance of war; or, if she is supposed to be too proud to be governed by her sense of interest, that her honour was concerned in the keeping up of

* The National Assembly had probably been deceived respecting the sentiments of the people of this country, but previous to the war they had discovered their error. The decree of the 19th November might perhaps be somewhat influenced by their notion of the existence of a republican spirit here, and in this respect the addresses from different bodies of Englishmen did great mischief. But the effects of the proclamation had shewn the real temper of the nation in a clear and striking light, and this was well understood in France when they were negociating for peace.

† See the Letters of M. Le Brun to Lord Grenville, Star, 22d May.

hostilities,

hoftilities, or her paffions gratified by the continuance of deftruction.

It is well known that the treaty of Pillnitz was the fource of all the prefent hoftilities; and it might have been forefeen that an attempt to carry it into effect would produce a great part of the calamities which have enfued. At the time that this took place, the conftitution of France was fettled; the king and the people had fworn to obey it. There was in it a good deal to praife, and much to blame; but, for reafons which it would be ufelefs to detail, it was on the whole impracticable. The men of talents and influence in France had however feen their error in weakening the executive power too much; they were rallying round the throne; and the army, headed by the pureft and moft popular character in the nation, were acquiring every day more and more military habits and virtues. The conftitution, with all its faults, had produced the moft fenfible advantages to the labouring part of the people *; it contained within itfelf the means of correcting both its principles and practice; and there was perhaps a chance that thefe might have been remedied without a civil war. It is however far more probable that a civil war muft have enfued; but if the parties had been left to themfelves, there is no one will deny that Fayette and his friends, in poffeffion of all the conftitutional authorities, would in all human probability have been victorious, and the ill-fated monarch have preferved his life and his crown. In the mean time the reft of Europe might have refted in peace—the conftitution, modelled perhaps on our own, would have affumed a more practicable and confiftent form, and liberty been eftablifhed on law.

The danger to which the final triumph of the new conftitution was expofed, arofe from a foreign war If the neigh-

* See the Tour of Mr. Arthur Young.

bouring

bouring nations fhould attempt an invafion of France for the avowed purpofe of reftoring its ancient government, from that inftant it was evident that the conftitution and the king himfelf were in extreme hazard. By the conftitution, the whole means of the nation's defence againft this invafion muft be trufted in the hands of the king himfelf, to replace whom in unlimited power the invafion was made. Among a people intoxicated with liberty, and jealous in the extreme, it was impoffible that any wifdom could in fuch circumftances fecure an already fufpected monarch from the imputation of treachery. As the danger from this treachery became greater, the paffions of the people arofe ; when the Duke of Brunfwick entered France, they burft into open infurrection, and through a fcene of dreadful flaughter the conftitution was overturned, and the monarch dethroned. This crifis was forefeen by the Jacobins, and by every means provoked ; it was forefeen by the Feuillans (the true friends of liberty and of limited monarchy), and earneftly deprecated. The virtuous monarch himfelf was fenfible of his danger, and in his extreme diftrefs applied to England to avert it. It was evident that the Emperor would not venture on this invafion without the aid of our ally the king of Pruffia, who had no more pretence for attacking France, than for his invafion of Poland, in which fuch flagrant wickednefs and fuch deteftable hypocrify have been openly difplayed. The unhappy Louis intreated our interference to detach the king of Pruffia from his defign, in language the moft preffing and moft pathetic. Such an opportunity of exerting great power on a moft fublime occafion, and to the nobleft of purpofes, is not likely to recur in a fingle age, and is referved by providence for its choiceft favourites. Such an opportunity was prefented to you, and you weakly and blindly caft it away.

The language which you put into your fovereign's mouth on that occafion is on record.—Profeffing every good
with

wifh for the king of France, mankind were then told, that the king of England could not interfere, unlefs he was requefted by all the parties concerned; that is, not only by him in diftrefs, but by thofe alfo whofe conduct occafioned the danger! The confpirators at Pilfnitz, and the Jacobins of Paris, equally triumphed on this occafion.— The conftitution and liberties of France were the objects of their common attack. At the fame inftant foreign war and internal infurrection fell with all their furies on the friends of the king, of law, and of order ; the ftreets and the prifons of Paris overflowed with their blood ; and thofe who efcaped the daggers of the Jacobins were feized on the frontier by our ally of Pruffia, loaded with chains, and fent to the dungeon of Magdeburg, to perifh in filence, or fuffer in hopelefs captivity worfe than death can inflict. Gratified in the deftruction of their common enemy, the votaries of fuperftition and of enthufiafm have met in dreadful conflict ; a war of unexampled fury has enfued ; and after the facrifice of a hundred thoufand lives, the flower of the youth of France and Germany, the hoftile armies are precifely in the fame fituation as when the carnage began!

Another opportunity had in the mean time offered for England to interfere, and to reftore the peace of Europe.— Winter produced a temporary fufpenfion of hoftilities. It is well known that Pruffia, baffled and worn out, wifhed, during this armiftice, to make its peace with France, and that Spain was about to fettle its difference with her alfo. Auftria, left alone, was unequal to the conteft, and by our mediation peace might have been reftored.— Difficulties had indeed occurred : France had not only repelled her invaders, but had in her turn become the aggreffor, and Flanders had been over-run by the arms of the victorious republic. The poffeffion of Flanders by France might not only weaken Auftria too much (I ufe the language of politicians), but expofe Holland

land to be invaded and over-run—France muſt therefore be
induced to renounce Brabant. In the mean time there were
new difficulties in the way of negociating with France, from
the change which had taken place in its government. Thoſe
who had hardly been able to ſee with patience the repreſen-
tative of the conſtitutional king, could not be expected to receive with kindneſs the delegate of the new republic. If
however we treated at all, it muſt be with thoſe who held the
reins of government, men, it muſt be acknowledged, againſt
whom the feelings of almoſt every heart in England revolted.
A miniſter is, however, to conſult his reaſon, not his feelings,
and to liſten only to the intereſts of his country. If theſe
require peace, his duty is to procure it by every fair and rea-
ſonable means; and, if he treats at all, to treat with temper,
even though his opponents are *robbers in their cave*. If war,
on the other hand, be inevitable, his buſineſs is evident—to
refuſe all negociation, and to let looſe the whole force of the
ſtate. You took a middle courſe: the dangers of war could
not be altogether overlooked. You would treat therefore,
but under a delicate diſtinction, which was to appear to our
allies as if we did not treat at all; and, as it ſhould ſeem, to
ſecure your honour, you ſet out in the buſineſs with *refuſing
the right of your antagoniſts to hold a treaty*. Le Brun and his
aſſociates however ſubmitted; it is known that they were
ready to have renounced Brabant, rather than go to war with
England; and univerſal peace was perhaps once more in
your power. By this time however the nation was inflamed
to a great degree by the apprehenſion of internal conſpi-
racies; and the dreadful anathemas of Mr. Burke in the
houſe of commons had deſtroyed all temper and moderation.
From Mr. Fox the mention of peace with France had been
received almoſt with execration, and England was pervaded
with the ſpirit of the ancient cruſades. In this ſituation every
moment became more critical—you heſitated—negociation

was

was one day begun and the next abandoned—Standing on the brink of a precipice, you dallied with the temper of two inflamed nations, and were pufhed forwards into this bloody war. If you did not act as a great ftatefman on this occafion, fome apology may be found for you—your temper was perhaps irritated; your fenfe of honour and your feelings of fympathy outraged; and though the minifter cannot be pardoned, the man may ftand excufed. Deeply as I lament the war and its confequences, I muft fairly admit, that the madnefs of the moment renders it doubtful, whether it could have been avoided during the laft days of negociation, by any meafures in your power. Indecifion is certainly not a part of your character in feafons of difficulty or danger; but on this occafion it feems fairly to be imputed to you; and to this it was owing that the *alarmifts* had taken the nation out of your hands.

Without imputing bad motives to thofe who ftood forward to propagate the rumours of internal fedition and confpiracy on that occafion, it may now, I think, be faid pretty confidently, that their fears greatly magnified the real danger. Why they were terrified, and why their terrors were in a great meafure vain, may be eafily underftood by any one acquainted with human nature, who looks at all the events of that period with an impartial eye. The retreat of the Duke of Brunfwick, the battle of Jemappe, and the conqueft of Flanders came fo rapidly and fo unexpectedly upon us, that men who had blindly wifhed, and weakly predicted, the immediate fubjugation of France to the Pruffian arms, were feized with a fudden terror proportioned to their foolifh hopes. France, marching with giant ftrides over her frontier, feemed to threaten the world. Thofe who in the firft inftance had not taken into their calculation the force of enthufiafm acting on a great and powerful nation in a moment of external invafion, could not, it may reafonably be fuppofed, form any

juft

juſt opinion of its nature or extent ; and ſaw in their fright-
ened imaginations, not only the downfall of the deſpotic
governments of Europe, but **the** overthrow of our own happy conſtitution, the **ſource of** ſo many bleſſings, and the well-
earned purchaſe of more than one revolution, and of many
years of civil **war.** On the other hand, the ſurpriſing ſuc-
ceſs of the French raiſed to a high elevation of ſpirits all
thoſe **who,** from whatever motives, had intereſted themſelves
in their favour ; and the claſſic grace with which **the ſpear**
of Liberty was wielded at Jemappe, threw a momentary veil
over former proceedings, too foul to bear the light. In this
ſituation of things, it was impoſſible that parties feeling ſo
differently ſhould not be mutually offenſive to each other,
and that thoſe who triumphed for the moment ſhould not
become ſubjects of apprehenſion to thoſe already ſo dread-
fully alarmed.

During this ſtate of jealous fear, ſtrong confirmations
could not be wanting, for " trifles light as air" would have
ſerved the purpoſe ; and it is well known, that even the very
looks of the ſuppoſed republicans were ſtated in the houſe
of commons as proofs of their ſeditious views. It muſt however be acknowledged, that there were great folly and indiſ-
cretion, to ſay no worſe, in the conduct of many of the *new
Whigs* * ; and that the addreſſes to the National Aſſembly
from ſocieties in England, however they might be intended,
were incapable of producing any good, and were pregnant with
the moſt ſerious evils. Whether any thing reſembling a plot
really exiſted, cannot perhaps be as yet aſcertained. Floating
notions of change probably pervade the imaginations, and
occaſionally eſcaped the lips of enthuſiaſts ; but it does not
appear at all likely that any plan for this purpoſe was con-

---

* This deſcription of men has not yet got a name that both they and their
opponents admit—Patriots and Jacobins are the parts deſignations—I chooſe
a middle term, and quote for this appellation the authority of Mr. Burke.

cented

certed or even meditated in any quarter. And the notion fo industrioufly circulated, that there was among us a large body of men, fome of them of the firft talents, leagued in a confpiracy againft their country with the Jacobin party of France, is one of thofe wild and " foolifh things," of which in a few months thofe who credited it " will in their cooler moments be afhamed," and which will foon be remembered only for mifchief it has done.

It is to this general fufpicion that the war itfelf is in great meafure to be attributed. One part of the cabinet, as report fays, was warmly and decidedly for it from the firft ; and the eagernefs of the *Alarmifts* in the houfe of commons in favour of this bloody meafure is well known. A ftep fo fatal to the general interefts of the country would not, however, have been taken in the face of even a feeble oppofition out of doors. Three public meetings—at Manchefter, Wakefield, and Norwich, prevented the Ruffian war. But where was oppofition now to come from ? Every man that objected to a meafure of minifters was by this time fuppofed to be an enemy to the conftitution ; and he who oppofed a war with France, was openly cried down as a fecret ally of the Jacobins, and as only anxious to fave them from the force of our irrefiftible arm. Profeffions of attachment to our own happy conftitution were regarded as of no value, unlefs they were accompanied with a blind and unlimited confidence in adminiftration ; and he only was confidered as a true friend to his country, who was ready to put all our bleffings at hazard, by rufhing madly forward into this foolifh crufade.

The whole body that affociated with Mr. Reeves feemed to think the fupport of the war neceffary to the fupport of the conftitution ; and in the houfe of commons Mr. Burke, with the peculiar phrenfy that diftinguifhes all his conduct, reiterated the war-hoop of *atheifm*, and pronounced Mr. Fox's propofal of attempting to avert hoftilities by negociation, as

a ftep

a step that would by neceſſary conſequence expoſe our virtuous monarch, with little proſpect of eſcape, to the fate of the unfortunate Louis *.

It was owing I preſume to the ſyſtem you have adopted, that though, as it has ſince appeared, you were at this time actually negociating, you preſerved a cautious ſilence, and ſuffered the nation to believe you thought with Mr. Burke. For the firſt time in his life Engliſhmen were in ſympathy with this extraordinary character, and madneſs became more contagious than the plague.

If it were at all proper to argue with men who can believe that the only means of ſecuring the reverence of the nation for the conſtitution, is to plunge us into all the horrors and miſeries of a foreign war, I would point out the conſequences that may poſſibly reſult from the rebound of general ſentiment, from the union of ſtarving ignorance with deſperate ambition, and from the progreſs of poverty, miſery, and diſcontent. But I do not think it neceſſary at preſent to inſiſt on ſuch topics; becauſe, blindly and fooliſhly as ſuch men have acted on their own principles, I believe the ſeaſon

* The manner in which this ſtrange man has introduced his ſovereign into debate, at different times, is truly curious. His conduct in this reſpect during the regency, when he repreſented the Almighty as having hurled him from his throne—and at the time now alluded to, when, in the exceſs of his loyalty, he expreſſed his fears of his being beheaded—are apparently much contraſted, but evidently flow from the ſame ſtructure of mind. A man that could talk openly in the houſe of commons of the " King's head being cut off," is not, however, I apprehend, likely to be appointed a lord of the bed-chamber, or even a gentleman-uſher. Mr. Burke, it is ſaid, is a poet; and this is true. But there ſeems about him a phrenſy that is more than poetical—an habitual diſpoſition to exaggeration, that treſpaſſes the bounds, not of truth only, but of nature—and an iraſcibility that has no reſemblance to any thing to be ſeen in rational life, and that impreſſes upon us the notion of a mind diſeaſed! In this view of the ſubject Mr. Burke is perhaps an object of pity. When his fits are not upon him, he is known to be gentle and humane.

of

of delufion is paffing, and that Englifhmen will be able to
diftinguifh, under every event, the fubftantial excellence of
our conftitution ; and attribute their fufferings, whatever they
may be, to their own delufion, and the madnefs of thofe who
have mifled the public mind.

But it may be faid that the war is likely to be fhort and
fuccefsful, and is therefore now to be perfifted in, however
indifcreetly it may have been begun.

The anfwer to this is not difficult—The war has had
already all the fuccefs that we could hope for : it brought on
the invafion of Holland, and that invafion is repelled : it has
obliged the French to abandon Flanders—to do that by force,
which they were before inclined to do by negociation : it has
covered the fea with our fhips of war, and made the mer-
chantmen both of France and England difappear—and finally,
after feveral hard fought battles, it has enabled the king of
Pruffia to lay fiege to Mentz, and the Prince of Coburg to fit
down before Valenciennes—But what is really of importance,
it has brought from the French new offers of peace.

What then may be the caufe why we fo proudly and
fullenly (as it is faid) reject them ?

It may be faid, that we wifh to carry on the war till we
obtain a barrier againft the future irruptions of the French
into Holland or Brabant ; and that, this being effected, we
mean with our allies to reft on our arms, and leave the nation
to fettle its own government. If this be our policy, it were far
better to reft now.

The probability of obtaining and of preferving peace
depends, in a great meafure, on the terms which are offered
according with natural principles of equity. That every nation fhould keep within its own confines, and choofe its own
government, without molefting its neighbours, is a propofi-
tion which is agreeable to our common apprehenfions of
juftice ; and, applied fairly and equally to the powers at war,

it

it may produce a speedy and lasting peace. But to insist, as a ground-work of such a treaty, that the Austrians shall obtain and keep possession of those strong fortresses on the northern frontier by which France is defended, is to propose that which is equally offensive to the pride and alarming to the fears of Frenchmen, and which is likely to occasion a vast and a fruitless effusion of human blood. " Shall we consent (they will cry) that France shall be dismembered? Shall we abandon our countrymen of Lisle and Valenciennes to the despots of Germany? If we give up a part of our territory, what security shall we have that the dividers of Poland will rest contented with a part, especially when, by possessing our strong holds, they may invade us at pleasure, and march at once into the heart of our defenceless country?" Such are the questions that will be asked, and it must be acknowledged that they are founded on natural feelings and reasonable fears : before these are subdued, many a brave man will perish in the field. But if indeed the security of the Low Countries be our only object, why not fortify Namur, Mons, Tournay, &c. which the Emperor Joseph dismantled, under an idea (which illustrates very strongly the folly of attempting to look far into futurity) that the marriage of his sister with the unfortunate Louis would render a barrier needless on the side of France? If those fortifications which were thought sufficient against Louis XIV. are not sufficient against the proud republicans, why not erect others? and if bankrupt Austria cannot do this, let us (if we must mingle in their affairs) be taxed to support them, but let it be for an expenditure that will terminate in peace.

The real interest of foreign nations is not, whether France shall have a constitution of this or that form; it is, that she shall have a regular government of some form or other, which may secure the faith of treaties, and due subordination to law; and this is the interest of the people of France themselves themfelves more than any other. Why then, it may be faid, do they not follow their intereft? Becaufe they do not perceive it; and they are prevented from perceiving it by the preffure of external war.

Revolutions of government call forth great talents and virtues, but they alfo too frequently call forth great crimes. Where all the ufual ordinances of law and fociety are broken down, men will rife indeed in fome degree according to their activity and powers, but in a degree too according as thefe are exerted without fcruple or reftraint. In the enthufiaftic ftate of mind by which revolutions are accompanied, great crimes make little impreffion on the *million*, provided they are committed in the fpirit of party, and under the appearance of patriotifm. Compaffion, charity, candour, and even a fenfe of juftice, are too generally fwept away in the whirlwind of paffion and prejudice, and lie buried under the wreck of virtuous habits and principles, to revive in quieter times. In fuch a ftate of things the natural influence of integrity and property, as well as the artificial diftinctions of rank and birth, give way to the governing power of enthufiafm; and men often rife to direction and command from the loweft ftations, by the force of ftrong talents and bold tempers, and by the buoyancy of heated imaginations.

Enthufiafm is in feafons of danger felt by virtuous as well as by unprincipled minds—by the former indeed perhaps more than the latter: but in virtuous minds, while it expands all the generous feelings, it does not deftroy the reftraints of principle or honour, even towards antagonifts or enemies, and much lefs towards thofe embarked in the fame caufe.

Revolutions however, in their progrefs, ftir up fociety more and more, even to the very dregs, and bring forward more and more of ignorance and profligacy (terms which in political life are nearly convertible) into the general mafs of

feeling

feeling and of action, in which the national will and the national force reside. Men who wish to guide this will, and direct this force, in times of popular commotion, must partake of its character, and vary their conduct with the rapid changes which the general sentiment undergoes. But in every great revolution this sentiment has a tendency to become gradually worse, and the character of those at the helm must become worse also. In the course of this melancholy progress, therefore, men of real principle and pure honour, who cannot bend to the opinions of the day, are probably thrown off, or perhaps destroyed, and are succeeded by other descriptions, each in succession more unlike the first, till at last perhaps the unprincipled and desperate obtain undisputed sway.

Hence, in our own country, the resistance to Charles I. which was led by Hampden and Faulkland, terminated in Cromwell and Lambert: and hence the revolution of France, originating with Fayette, Neckar, and Mirabeau, has descended into the hands of Danton and Robespierre *.

The

* The American revolution may be instanced as an exception to this general representation, but improperly. We must first observe (as was noticed by Mr. Fox in his speech on Mr. Grey's motion) that in America, though there was a change of the governing power, there was no revolution of habits or opinions—no sudden change of principles. It must be observed also, that the Americans had much less of poverty and ignorance among them (though less knowledge no doubt) than what is to be found in England and France. And thirdly, it must be observed, that something of the same kind did actually take place in America as in England and France, though certainly in a less degree. Round the American Revolution, as well as the American character, a false glare has been thrown by the splendour of their success. The congress did not, like the national assembly, expose their debates and dissensions to their own people, much less to all Europe; but it is well known that a party prevailed in it to a considerable degree, and Washington himself, if report speaks truth, was at one time preserved in his command by a single vote only. In the course of the revolution many bloody deeds were acted, the memory of which need not now be revived. But the

following

The influence however of men who openly violate the first obligations, as well as the most palpable interests of society, is exposed to continual danger from the very scaffolding on which it is raised, and cannot survive that heated and enthusiastic state of mind which extinguishes for a time, and for a time only, the feelings of compassion and the sense of justice.

Enthusiasm is, from its very violence, of short continuance: it produces the most cruel desolations in society: but, as Mr Hume has observed, " its fury is like that of thun- " der and tempest, which exhaust themselves in a little time, " and leave the air more calm and serene than before." The accounts that we receive of the French shew clearly, that they are at present a nation of enthusiasts: of this their very crimes give the most decided evidence. Their contempt of danger and hardships; their utter disregard of self-interest, and of all the motives which influence men in tranquil life;

following quotation from the history of the American revolution by Dr. Ram- say, himself a member of the congress, will shew how the morals of the people were affected, and bear testimony to the author's candour and love of truth. " Time and industry have already, in a great degree, repaired the losses of " property which the citizens sustained during the war, but both have " hitherto failed in effacing the taint which was then communicated to " their principles; nor can its total ablution be expected till a new gene- " ration arises, unpractised in the iniquities of their fathers." If indeed Dr. Ramsay had not acknowledged this, the conduct of the assemblies which were elected immediately after the revolution would sufficiently prove it. By these assemblies standing on a popular basis (especially by that of South Carolina) acts were passed dissolving the obligations of justice in a way as arbitrary, and nearly as open, as those of the most despotic monarch what- ever. An experience of the evils resulting from such outrages has reformed both the principles and the practice of the American politicians; and men of honour and integrity, many of them beaten down by the revolution, have recovered their proper influence in quieter times. Over and above all the circumstances I have mentioned, the natural phlegm of the American character, compared with the vehemence and impetuosity of the French, was an advantage not to be calculated.

their

their frantic fchemes; their wild fufpicions; their implaca-
bility towards their enemies; their pronenefs to murder;—
thefe are the true and exact features of enthufiafm, operat-
ing on minds previoufly degraded by a fuperftition the moft
vile, and by a flavery the moft abject *.

The more fiercely this national difeafe rages, the more
certainly will it terminate fpeedily, provided it be left to itfelf. Society cannot poffibly fubfift under the prefent fyftem
in France, and the exceffes of the Jacobins muft fooner or
later produce their deftruction. The nation, waking from
its delirium, will fee the horror of its fituation, and fly for a
refuge from anarchy to the conftitution it has rejected, or fome
better regulated form of government; or perhaps to the very
defpotifm it has overthrown. But, if continued attacks are
made from without, this iffue will certainly be prolonged,
and may perhaps be prevented, till the defpotic governments
now in arms, every day becoming more poor, and therefore
more oppreffive, fhall be themfelves brought to the ground!

The great inftrument of the fuccefs of the Jacobins has
been the fufpicion they have conftantly excited, that every
friend of peace and fubordination was connected with the
foreign enemies that are invading France †. A high-fpirited
nation will not receive the pureft of bleffings on compulfion,

* In Dr. Moore's Journal, various proofs of the truth of this may be
found.—A Sans Culotte prefenting to the National Affembly, on the 10th of
Auguft, the head of a murdered Swifs, and at the fame time emptying out of
his hat the jewels and gold which he had found in the Thuilleries, is a ftrik-
ing picture of the fpecies of difeafe of mind under which the nation labours.

† The ftrength of fuch an inftrument as this may be judged of by the
fuccefs with which it was employed by the *alarmifts* here. The friends of
peace in this country were in the fame manner denounced as leagued with
foreign invaders; and this was the real fecret of Meffrs. Reeves, Burke, and
Co. for *levelling the levellers*, at the fuccefs of which, confidering the men,
many people have been fo much furprifed. The nation was panic-ftruck,
and apprehenfion and credulity go hand in hand.

H . and

and would reject the British conftitution itfelf, though it were abfolutely perfect, if prefented on the bayonet's point. But what boon do the conquerors of Poland hold out to them? What bleffings do the people of Germany offer to their view? Abfolute fubjugation to a foreign force is the favour and the mercy of the rulers; ignorance and fubmiffion to unlimited oppreffion is the example of the armed flaves whom they command. It is no wonder that a nation of enthufiafts fhould be inflamed to madnefs on the approach of fuch invaders, and, fpurning the dictates of reafon, fhould confider thofe who would reftrain them as leagued with their enemies, and commit themfelves to fuch only as are as frantic as themfelves. Hence every attempt to reftore order to France has been fruftrated by foreign invafion; Clermont-Tonnerre and Rochfoucauld have been murdered; and Narbonne, Fayette, and Liancourt have fled. And hence alfo it is but too likely that the fiege of Valenciennes and Condé will prove the ruin of the brave and perhaps honeft infurgents on the banks of the Loire. How certain the overthrow of the Jacobin fyftem in France would be, if the nation were left to itfelf, may be gathered, not only from the nature of that fyftem, but from the attempts to overturn it in the very face of a foreign invafion; and how very unlikely the allies are to fucceed in their endeavours to give a conftitution to France by force (the only rational object for which war can be continued), may be collected, not only from the hiftory of the paft, and from what has been already mentioned, but from other confiderations.

Under the preffure of external invafion, almoft any government will hold a nation together; and every form of republican government, however unfit for quieter feafons, is at fuch times productive of great energy of mind, and therefore of great national force. The caufe of this is to be traced to the peculiar confequence which a republican government gives

gives to the individual, by which his country becomes of confequence to him, and the whole ftrength of his private and public affections in a moment of external invafion bears on a fingle object—the national defence. The truth of this might be amply illuftrated from the hiftory of the republics of Greece and Rome; where may be feen alfo, what appears fo very extraordinary in modern times, the moft unbounded licentioufnefs and confufion in the centre of the government, joined with the moft formidable power on the frontiers*.

In times of peace the exiftence of primary affemblies, fuch as are univerfal in France, feems incompatible with the fafety of eftablifhed government; but in a fituation like the prefent, thefe will be the nurferies of courage, of eloquence, of daring minds;—by giving every individual an active and perfonal intereft in the ftate, they will ftrengthen its defence in an extraordinary manner. The divifion of France into diftricts and departments, eftablifhes within it fo many rival republics, and in this way will probably produce that high-fpirited emulation between neighbouring communities, fo dangerous to internal quiet, but to which Greece, when invaded, owed its fafety in the claffic ages, and perhaps Switzerland its independence in modern times.

In the progrefs of revolutions, it is material to obferve, that talents do not feem to fuffer an equal degradation with principles. On the contrary, fituations of continued difficulty and danger have a tendency to call them forth (in as far as

* In this refpect, as well as in feveral others, France recalls to our minds the ftates of antiquity. There are indeed circumftances of refemblance in their fituation that might afford room for much curious obfervation, and our hefitation in applying the experience we derive from Greece or Rome to modern France is perhaps chiefly founded on a doubt, which at times has appeared reafonable enough—whether thefe countries have contained beings of the fame fpecies—whether thefe French be indeed men, or fome other defcription of animals.

H 2

they

they are diftinct from virtue) more and more, and to
ftrengthen and expand them when found. In long eftablifhed monarchies, fuch as are fpread over the continent of
Europe, rank has the chief, or indeed the fole influence in
beftowing command, and nature in beftowing talents pays
no attention to rank. But in revolutions, artificial diftinctions being overturned, the order of nature is in fome degree
reftored, and talents rife to their proper level. Hence it is
that revolutions, once fet on foot, have the weight of talents
generally in their favour. It may be objected, indeed, that
when the fword is once drawn, the iffue depends on military
difcipline and fkill, and that thefe will always be found on
the fide of experience. Daily obfervation however proves,
that the mere mechanifm of a foldier is eafily and fpeedily
learnt; and the uniform voice of hiftory tells us, that the
qualities of a great general are in an efpecial manner the
work of nature; what fuperior genius feems to acquire the
foonest, and what all other men find it impoffible to acquire
at all. Hence, though in the beginning of wars difcipline
and eftablifhed rank have ufually the advantage, in the courfe
of them nature and genius always preponderate *.

* The whole of thefe obfervations might be illuftrated from our own
civil wars. Deteftable as Cromwell and his affociates were in many refpects,
they muft be allowed to have poffeffed very fuperior talents both in the cabinet and the field. In the beginning of the war, military experience was
entirely with the king; but, what is curious, there did not arife one good com-
mander on his fide, the gallant Montrofe excepted, and he, it may be obferved, was educated among the covenanters. On the other fide arofe Effex,
Fairfax, Cromwell, Ireton, Lambert, and Monk. Moft of thefe had no previous acquaintance with military affairs. Cromwell, the firft captain of the
age, was forty-three years old before he became a foldier. Thefe curious
circumftances have not efcaped Mr. Hume, nor the explanation of them.
Reflecting on this fubject, I have fometimes amufed myfelf with fuppofing
what fort of military commanders our political leaders would make, and I
apprehend they would arrange themfelves pretty much according to their
prefent order.—Firft-rate talents are of univerfal application.

The

The application of thefe obfervations to the affairs of France is fo obvious, that it would be fuperfluous, as well as tedious, to point it out.

The impoffibility of conquering opinions by the fword, and the dreadful flaughter which the attempt when perfifted in muft neceffarily occafion, may be learnt from the revolution in the Low Countries, and the bloody tranfactions which were there **carried on** under the direction of Alva. If the great mafs of the people have imbibed opinions, extermination **only** can root them out. Hence the *fundamentality* of the French revolution, fo much exclaimed againft by the weak and fearful, and fo much dreaded even by the enlightened, though it will probably be the fource of long internal diffentions, renders it invulnerable by foreign attack. Mr. Hume has remarked the univerfal and extreme reluctance with which men abandon power once poffeffed; and you, Mr. Pitt, can probably fpeak to this truth from your own feelings.—Well then, Sir, the Sans Culottes have recovered what they call their rights, and may be faid to be men in power—power newly tafted, after long and hard oppreffion. Whether this power be good for them or not is another thing—they think it good, and that is enough. When once they have obtained quiet poffeffion of it, they will probably abufe it, as other men in power have done before them. But while it is attempted to be wrefted from them by armed force, it will rife every moment in their eftimation, and death only will be able to rob them of their prize. The revolution of Poland, on the other hand, was not a *fundamental* revolution; and it was praifed by Mr. Burke (a fufpicious circumftance) on this account. The truth is, it was a change of the form of government, and a partial enlargement of its bafis, from which however nine tenths of the people of Poland were entirely fhut out. When the king and the nobles therefore abandoned it, the peafantry abandoned

abandoned it alfo, and found no motive for rifking their lives in defence of bleffings they had not been permitted to tafte. This is the real caufe of the rapid fuccefs of the confederate arms, and not the open plains and difmantled fortreffes of the country, as fome have fuppofed. The true defence of a nation in fuch circumftances—the only defence that is impregnable, lies in the poor man's heart;—that abandoned, the reft is eafy.

In viewing this fubject, fo many confiderations rufh on the mind to fhew the folly of the prefent invafion of France, that I am compelled to dwell on general topics only ; otherwife I might expatiate on the utter incapacity of the Auftrian army to keep the field at all without fupplies from this country, and the impoffibility of our finding fuch fupplies. Abject as the temper of the nation appears, it will not, I apprehend, fubmit to utter ruin ; and I pronounce coolly, what I have confidered deeply, that nothing but utter ruin can be the confequence of our perfifting in this copartnerfhip with the folly and bankruptcy of the continental powers. It is not enough that we pay with Englifh guineas, extracted from the labour of our oppreffed peafantry, the people of Heffe and Hanover, to fight German battles ; we muft fupport the armies of Auftria alfo, and, from the wreck of our ruined manufactures, fupply them with food, clothing, and arms. But what confummates our misfortunes is, that if by our affiftance the confederates fhould fucceed in their views, England will be blotted out of the fyftem of Europe : Holland cannot preferve her independence a fingle day ; a connected chain of defpotifm will extend over the faireft portion of the Earth ; and the lamp of Liberty, that has blazed fo brightly in our "Sea-girt Ifle," muft itfelf be extinguifhed in the univerfal night *.

The

* I purpofely avoid enlarging on this view of the fubject, becaufe I think nothing

The mifchief that is meditated is of a magnitude that feems more than mortal, but happily the execution of it requires more than mortal force. The ignorant and innocent flaves that are the inftruments on this occafion are men —they muft be clothed and fed—they have men to contend with, and are liable to the death they are fent to inflict—they may perifh by the fword, by fatigue, by famine, and by difeafe. The new Alarics that employ them are men alfo, weak, ignorant, and mortal like the reft. Death will foon level them with the inftruments of their guilty ambition. In a few years, or perhaps a few months, Catherine will fleep, lifelefs, with Jofeph, with Leopold, with *Peter the Third*. New characters lefs tinctured with prejudice will receive a portion of the fpirit of the age, the fyftems of defpotifm be broken, and mortality come in aid of reafon and truth.

In the mean time it is poffible that Condé and Valenciennes may be taken, and that the hoftile armies may march into France as before. If purfued into their own country, Frenchmen will, in all probability, continue united; and they will carry on the war, when compared to their affailants, at little expenfe. The men are on the fpot; their provifions are behind them; mufkets are in their hands; enthufiafm in their hearts. The more the nation is compreffed within its centre, the more will the elafticity of its force and courage increafe. The invaders will probably be again compelled to retreat, and their retreat will neither be eafy nor certain: the victorious republicans will purfue them, and again, perhaps, difdaining the reftraints of prudence, pufh their conquefts to the banks of the Rhine. A fingle action loft, a fingle action recovered, Flanders; and Flanders and Holland will now feel the fame blow.

nothing fo unlikely as the conqueft of France. It has been difcuffed in the Morning Chronicle, by a writer under the fignature of " A Calm Obferver," with a perfpicuity and force of reafoning that nothing can furpafs. The whole feries of letters far exceed any fimilar production of the Englifh prefs.

What

What shall save Holland if Flanders fall? The Cold-
stream you see are mortal men. Even the three princes of
the blood-royal of England will not appal the fierce republicans—*What care these roarers for the name of King** ? If the
danger I state seems at a distance, let it not on that account
be disregarded. Every step the allied armies advance into
France, the danger seems to me to approach; and were they
within ten leagues of Paris, I should tremble the more for
the fate of Amsterdam.

The opportunity of restoring general peace presented itself at the time of the congress of Antwerp. Dumourier had
retreated; Flanders was recovered. We had nothing to do
but to declare, what must I think be declared in the end,
that *if France will confine herself within her own territory, she
may there shape out her own constitution at her will.* Had this
been done at the time mentioned, Dumourier, not rendered
odious by foreign alliance, would in all probability have been
able to restore the constitutional monarchy; and in every
event, France, occupied by intestine divisions, would, as it
seems probable, have left Europe in quiet for many years to
come. This policy was so clear that a mere child might
have discerned it; it did not even require a negociation with
the French cabinet, and while it secured our best interests,
it left our honour without a stain.

How then shall we account for the resolves of the congress of Antwerp? We must unveil the truth. The members of this congress were German princes, or their agents;
even the representative of England there *was a German prince.*
Such men, from their education, are in general ignorant, and
labour under prejudices, from their situation, of a destructive
kind.

Military despots in their own dominions, they feel it their
personal interest, perhaps they think it the interest of mankind (such may be the force of prejudice) that despotism

* Shakespeare's Tempest.

should

should be univerfal. To fuch men the anarchy of France, under Jacobin rulers, is not half fo alarming as the conftitution to which this may give birth. They are aware that the crimes acting there at prefent are fufficient to render the French name deteftable among their fubjects; but if thefe crimes fhould open the eyes of the French themfelves—if, out of the mingled wrecks of defpotifm and anarchy, a limited monarchy fhould arife in France, as it did in England, or any other form of a free conftitution that fecures fubordination to law—then it is that the French example will become far more deftructive to arbitrary governments than their arms, and the crowned heads of Germany, great and fmall, will have real caufe to tremble. It is true, if they were enlightened, they need not tremble at all; they would fee that arbitrary power is as deftructive to him that poffeffes, as to him that endures it. But it cannot be expected that they fhould difcern this—the errors of education blind all but very fuperior minds; and though Germany produces more princes than all Europe befides, it is not once in a century that fhe produces a prince that is a truly great man*.

Mr. Fox contends that government is *from* the people; Mr. Wyndham that it is only *for* the people. Thefe philological diftinctions are not attended to by the rulers of Germany, among whom even the word *people* is not to be found. Their *fubjects*, they know, are accuftomed to obedience; the blefl-

* Frederick the Second was an extraordinary man, and it has amufed many perfons to fuppofe how he might have acted on the prefent occafion. This however feems pretty certain, that he would not have lain eight months in the neighbourhood of Mentz before he found an opportunity of laying fiege to it. The prefent conduct of the Pruffians conveys an eulogium on the talents of that great monarch, beyond the power of Hertzberg's oratory. As however they confidered themfelves facrificed before, their prefent backwardnefs may arife as much from fpleen as from any other caufe.

I

ings that flow from liberty and property they have never experienced, and they are therefore fit inſtruments in the hands of arbitrary power. Germany, it is well known, is inhabited chiefly by princes, nobles, muſicians, and peaſantry; merchants, manufacturers, and country gentlemen, the leading deſcriptions of Engliſhmen, are there almoſt wholly unknown. The three firſt of theſe claſſes are, during war, in their natural element; and the laſt, who ſuſtain all the evils and all the burthens, are as yet too abject and too ignorant to make their ſufferings dangerous to thoſe by whom they are oppreſſed. A perſeverance in the war will indeed deſtroy what little trade and manufactures there are in Germany, and render their governments (that of Hanover excepted, whoſe military expenſes are defrayed by England) univerſally bankrupt. The creditors of the ſtates will be ruined, but the expenſes of the courts and armies will not perhaps on that account be leſs. The ordinary revenue of a German prince depends chiefly on the products of the ſoil, and dreadful muſt be the oppreſſion indeed, before theſe fail. The peaſantry will be taxed more and more to ſupport increaſing burthens, and the extortion of ſuch taxes will rivet the poverty and ignorance through which alone theſe burthens are endured. It is thus that the tyranny of the rulers and the degradation of the people muſt keep equal pace; it is thus that deſpotiſm forms a natural alliance with ignorance, blaſts every charm of rational nature, and blunts every feeling of the human heart. There is indeed a point at which the oppreſſion of the moſt abject becomes no longer ſafe—a point to which, if I miſtake not, the deſpotic governments of Europe are faſt approaching. They have undertaken to ſubdue the enemies of kingly government in France, and are ſtaking their whole credit on the iſſue of an undertaking from which, according to every human appearance, they will return baffled and diſgraced. The moſt deſpotic

7
governments

governments depend for their exiſtence on opinion, as well as the moſt free. If the concert of princes ſhould be baffled, the prejudices of their ſubjects will be ſhaken, and the foundation of their thrones will from that moment be for ever inſecure.

Behold then, **once** more, a criſis which has ſo often occurred in hiſtory; which has preſented ſo frequent and ſo awful a warning to rulers, and has preſented it ſo often in vain! **A** government bankrupt by its own waſte and folly; ſenſible of its inſecurity, and therefore jealous, irritable, and oppreſſive. A people already labouring under almoſt intolerable burthens, and doomed to ſuffer others more heavy ſtill—caſting off, with its prejudices, the habitual ſubmiſſion and reſpect to its rulers, and imbibing thoſe immutable truths which are ſo dangerous to oppreſſors, and ſometimes indeed ſo fatal to thoſe who are oppreſſed. Every day **the** breach widens—the ſword at length is drawn, and the ſcabbard caſt away.—In the dreadful conflict which follows there is only one alternative; the government muſt be overturned, or the people reduced to the condition of beaſts. We cannot have forgotten the cauſes which have produced the revolutions of Switzerland, Holland, and England—which have ſo recently produced the revolution of France;—the ſame cauſes are again conſpiring to ſhake all Europe to its centre, and to form a new æra in human affairs.

What a dreadful infatuation is it which involves the fate of Engliſhmen in this impending ruin—which embarks our commerce, our manufactures, our revenue, perhaps our conſtitution itſelf, the ſource of all our bleſſings, in this deſperate cruſade of deſpotiſm and ſuperſtition againſt anarchy and enthuſiaſm! in the courſe of which, however it terminate, we can reap nothing but misfortune; and **in** the iſſue of which we may learn, that no human inſtitution **can** withſtand the folly of thoſe who adminiſter its powers.

Men

Men of Switzerland, how I respect you ! While the hurricane of human passions sweeps over France, Italy, and Germany, elevated on your lofty mountains, you are above the region of the storm. Secure in your native sense, your sincere patriotism, your simple government, your invincible valour, your eternal hills—you can look down on the follies and the crimes which desolate Europe, with calmness and with pity, and anticipate the happy æra when perhaps you may mediate universal peace. Sea-girt Britain might have enjoyed this situation, had she known how to estimate her blessings, and kept aloof from the madness of the day.

At this moment the session of parliament closes ;—a dead stillness prevails over England, the natural consequence of astonishment at the spreading destruction, and of strong passions violently suppressed. The Opposition, deserted by all those *feeble amateurs* whose minds have not sufficient comprehension to discern the true interest of their country, or whose nerves are too weak to bear up against vulgar prejudice, has endeavoured, but in vain, to discover the extent of our continental engagements, or the real objects of the war *. Two hundred and eighty members, ranging behind you, support every measure you propose ; and among the whole number, not a man has been found to inquire of you openly, in the name and in behalf of the people of England, how long their patience is to endure, and how far the progress of ruin is to extend?

You have assumed on this awful occasion the whole responsibility of public measures, and your character and reputation, I fear, you mistakingly conceive, are wholly committed on the successful issue of the war. Your real friends must

* Security and compensation are words that may be explained at pleasure.

sincerely

sincerely lament this on your own account; the friends of their country will lament it, on account of the general calamities it is likely to produce. The nation, Mr. Pitt, has loved you " well—not wisely;" and it is partly in consequence of this that at the present moment her real interests are opposed to the personal honour of him she has trusted and idolized. In this day of distress she is told to repose in the constitutional responsibility of ministers. " Be still, ye inhabi-" tants of the isle, thou whom the merchants of Zidon that " pass over the sea have replenished."—ISAIAH. Alas! what will silence do? Will the responsibility of ministers restore her ruined trade, feed her starving manufacturers? will it replace the husband and father to the widow or the orphan, or restore to the aged parent his gallant son? will it recall to life the brave men now mouldering in unhallowed earth in Flanders, joint-tenants of a common grave with those against whom they fought* ?

*　*　*　*　*　*

If I were bold enough to appreciate your political life, Mr. Pitt, I should be inclined to allow the outset of it extraordinary merit. The sentiment of approbation that attended you was indeed almost universal—you were the hope of the good, the pride of the wife, the idol of your country. If your official career had terminated with the discussions on the Regency, though one of the most fatal of your mistakes had been committed before this, it may be questioned whether modern Europe could have produced a politician or an orator more strenuous, more exalted, more authoritative†; one whose

* This affecting circumstance is, I am told, literally true.
† See Mr. Gratton's character of Lord Chatham, printed as Dr. Robertson's.

ambition was apparently more free from selfishness; who afforded to his opponents less room for censure, or gave to his friends more frequent occasions of generous triumph and honest applause.—The errors that you have fallen into, are natural for men long possessed of power uncontrolled; and in imputing them to you, I accuse you only of the weaknesses of human nature. It is not necessary to a free people to have rulers exempt from such weaknesses; but it is necessary for them to watch and to guard against these infirmities.

It is natural, I believe, for successful ambition to seek new objects on which it may exert itself. Hence, after you had subdued opposition in England, you issued forth like another Hercules in quest of new adventures, and traversed the continent of Europe to seek monsters whom you might subdue. You could not however but be sensible, that the reputation of a minister of trade and finance, which you had justly obtained, was incompatible with that of a great war minister in the present state of the nation. You took therefore the middle line; you made preparations for fighting on every occasion, but you took care not to strike. England might perhaps bear the expense of arming, but could not actually go to war; and this secret, which your three successive armaments discovered to all Europe, led Mirabeau on his death-bed to give you the name of *ministre preparatif.*

In men long in possession of power, a secret sympathy (unknown perhaps to themselves) is gradually strengthening in favour of others in the same situation, and a secret prejudice, amounting perhaps at last to enmity, against opposition to power in every form. Hence the danger you saw to England in the triumph of the patriots of Holland over the Prince of Orange, and the safety we acquired from the subjugation of the Dutch by the Prussian arms.—Hence also the perfect composure with which you expected the conquest

queft of France by the defpots of Germany, and the fudden
alarm with which you were feized, on the repulfion of that
invafion, and the overrunning of Flanders by the republican
arms. By the freedom of Brabant the conftitution of
England might be endangered; but it became the more fecure in your eye, it fhould feem, by the extenfion of defpotifm
over every corner of Europe, and the fuccefs of foreign bay-
onets in rooting out *liberty* as well as licentioufnefs in
France.

It is alfo to the unhappy prejudices of your fituation that
I attribute your want of moderation of temper on occafions of
the utmoft moment; your allying your great talents with the
weak judgments and violent paffions of thofe around you ; and
your blindnefs (if fuch it be) to the real dangers of this commercial nation, and to the path of fafety and of true honour,
which it was no lefs your duty than your intereft to purfue.

In contemplating events of fuch magnitude as thofe
connected with the French revolution, the utmoft calmnefs,
as well as comprehenfion of mind, is required—and more
particularly required in him who directs the affairs of a
great nation. Unhappily thefe qualities are feldom found in
any ftation; and this revolution, feen in part only, has become
the object of wild encomium, or of bitter reprobation, as the
prejudices of men have been affected, or their fympathies engaged. The moft prudent part perhaps for one whofe political fituation is influenced by the opinions he is fuppofed to
hold, is to be filent on the fubject. It is uncertain how this
extraordinary event may terminate, and its ultimate effects on
the human race cannot yet be afcertained. At prefent, however, it is well known, that not in England only, but in every
part of Europe, the dreadful exceffes in Paris, and elfewhere,
have turned the tide of popular fentiment and opinion
ftrongly againft the French. Even under the moft defpotic
governments, the people at prefent hug their chains, and
tyranny

tyranny itself is secure. Can it then be suppofed, that in England there is any ferious danger from the contagion of French principles; in England, where the conftitution is fo fubftantially good, and the people fo loyal and united? The theological and fectarian prejudices of different and oppofite kinds through which the affairs of France have been viewed, have indeed contributed moft fatally to bewilder the under-ftanding, and to inflame the prejudices of Englifhmen; and to thefe is to be imputed, in a great degree, that moft fingular delufion—that the fafety of our conftitution has depended on our rifking all our bleffings in this moft fruitlefs, expenfive, and bloody war. That delufion (for fuch I confider it) is now I hope nearly over; and peace, which is the general in-tereft, will foon, I doubt not, be the univerfal wifh. Every confideration calls loudly for it; and it may be much more eafily obtained now, when our enemies are humbled, and the people of England are ftill patient and filent, than at a future period, when the invading armies may be checked or repulfed, and the nation is become openly impatient under the expenfe and ruin of the war. A man of your fagacity will eafily dif-cern, that in times like the prefent, the gale of popular opi-nion is conftantly fhifting the point whence it blows, and will fee that it cannot be trufted to carry you forward in your prefent courfe, in the face of great and increafing obftacles.

The prefent ftate of affairs in this country, and on the continent of Europe, forms a fubject too interefting to be left without reluctance—but far too extenfive to be thoroughly inveftigated within the limits of a letter like this. The events of the day that is paffing are likely to affect every portion of Europe, and, in their confequences, the condition of the human race throughout the habitable earth. Many of the "bearings and ties" of this important fubject I have been obliged to neglect, and others I have only glanced at; for I write on the fpur of the occafion, and under difficulties and

interruptions

interruptions of various kinds. Should what I have written have the fortune to reach you, you will fee that it is addreffed to you more " in forrow than in anger," and on that account alone that it is not wholly unworthy of your regard. But I would farther perfuade myfelf, that it may fuggeft topics for ferious reflection, by impreffing on your mind the progrefs and unexampled extenfion of the war-fyftem throughout Europe; the correfponding progrefs of the funding-fyftem; the crifis to which this laft has in fome countries reached, and is every where approaching; and the probable as well as certain effects of this on our own commercial nation, and on mankind at large.

Hitherto you have taken it for granted, that though there is a certain point of depreffion to which the commerce of this country may fink in confequence of the war, yet that from this, as in former wars, it will naturally return. I have fuggefted to you, that this fuppofition is dangerous, as well as fallacious, from the increafed progrefs of our debts and taxes, from the locking up of the capital of our manufacturers in foreign debts, and from the growing poverty as well as the general bankruptcy that fpreads over Europe, in confequence of the continued preffure of former burthens, and the unexampled extent and expenfe of the prefent war. I have not ftated to you, under this head, the effects of a rapidly finking revenue, or of the emigration of our people to America; becaufe thefe confiderations are fo extremely ferious that they cannot be mentioned without grief and alarm, and may form, of themfelves, a very ample fubject for feparate difcuffion.

Mr. Dundas told us, in the houfe of commons, that our commercial diftreffes arofe from our extraordinary profperity, and boafted that all the world united with us in the war againft France. I have fhewn that his affertion is a poor fophifm, and his boaft a fubject of forrow and apprehenfion.

Mr. Wyndham expreffed his acquiefcence in the lofs of

K   our

our commerce, if we might retain our conftitution; and on the fame ground of preferving our conftitution, this perilous war has been often defended by yourfelf, your followers, and a great part of the nation. I have made out to you, what I know not how, as chancellor of the exchequer, you can well be ignorant of, that our commerce and our conftitution have a moft intimate dependence on each other; and that when the union is formed by twenty-four millions of taxes, tythes, and poor-rates, and two hundred and fifty millions of debt, they may be confidered as embarked in the fame adventure, and as likely to perifh in the fame ftorm.

How the war commenced I have endeavoured to explain, and you will confider in your calmer moments, whether you really exerted yourfelf to preferve peace by negociation, inftead of procuring it by arms; and to what profit you have turned the honeft affection of your countrymen for their conftitution and king, and the generous indignation with which they furveyed the madnefs and brutality of their neighbours.

On various occafions during this bloody conteft I have fhewn that the peace of Europe was in our power; that it was in our power recently on the retreat of Dumourier, and after we ourfelves had tafted the calamities of war. Why it was rejected you muft yourfelf explain;—I have defcribed the congrefs at Antwerp, and am no farther mafter of the fubject.

The views that you conceal cannot be afcertained, but what you have actually performed is not liable to mifapprehenfion. I have fuggefted to you, that you have united Englifhmen in the interefts and in the councils of thofe who formed the treaty of Pillnitz; who retain Fayette in chains; who were the real caufe of the triumphs of the Jacobin party in France over limited monarchy; who are in fact the pretext that the prefent anarchifts

have

have employed, and will employ, to juftify their defperate proceedings; and who, by their recent conduct in Poland, have given fuch proofs of their ambition, as well as of their power, as muft fill the heart of every friend of his fpecies with horror and alarm. That the deftroyers of the conftitution of Poland can be friendly to our own, the model on which it was formed, no one will believe. They are the deadly foes of liberty throughout the world; and I might have fhewn you, that in the deftruction of our revenue and commerce, the bulwarks will be removed which fecure us from their overwhelming force. I might alfo have pointed out the danger of fending our army to fight under their banners, and our princes to affociate in their councils;—but there are fentiments of ferious alarm which a lover of his country muft deeply feel, that in this feafon of delufion it may be dangerous to utter.

Of the two motives for continuing the war, fecurity and compenfation, I have confidered that which alone I can underftand, the former; and have fhewn that the attempt to take and to feparate from France its frontier towns on the north, is full of difficulty and hazard, and that while it may render the war doubly bloody and defperate, it can afford no fecurity beyond what might be obtained from fortifying Auftrian Flanders, already in our power. The true fecurity to this country arifing from the fettlement of the French government, I have endeavoured to fhew, is not promoted, but abfolutely prevented by the prefent invafion, which, fhould it be repelled, may leave unfortified Brabant, as well as Holland, an eafy conqueft to the republican arms.

In the fearful tragedy which is now acting on the theatre of Europe, you have unhappily made England one of the perfons of the drama, and fhe cannot but act a part of unparalleled importance. You have affumed the direction of this

K 2

part

part to yourself, and before parliament again meets, the hopes
and the fears of the enlightened, and the real interests of at
least the present race of mankind, may be at issue on your
single counsels. More than one false step you have already
made—the precipice is directly in your path, that leads to
inevitable destruction. I know the temptations and the difficulties of your situation—we will forget the past, but if you
advance, how shall you be forgiven?

In considering the aspect of the present times, I am sometimes affected with deep melancholy; yet I am not one of
those who despair of the fortunes of the human race.
Through the thick clouds and darkness that surround us, I
discern the workings of an over-ruling mind. Superstition I
know is the natural offspring of ignorance, and governs in
the dark ages with a giant's strength.—Unassisted reason is a
feeble enemy: opposed to superstition, reason, in days of ignorance, is a dwarf. In the order of providence, enthusiasm
arises to resist superstition—to combat a monster with a monster's force. What did Erasmus in the days of Luther?
What would Lowth have done in the days of Wycliffe, or
Blair in those of Knox? In the councils of Heaven, mean
and wicked instruments are often employed for the highest
purposes. The authors of the reformation were many of them
ignorant, fierce, and even bloody: but the work itself was of
the most important and most universal benefit to the human
race. The *despotism* of priests then received its death-wound,
and the *despotism* of princes has now perhaps sustained a
similar blow.—Pure religion has survived and improved after
the first; the true science of government may improve after
the last, and be built every where on the solid foundations of
utility and law. Before such happy consequences ensue, dreadful commotions may indeed be expected over Europe, commotions which England, and perhaps England only, may, if
she

she is wife, escape. The present generation will probably be swept away before the intellectual earthquake subsides; but those who succeed them, will, I trust, find the air more pure and balmy, and the skies more bright and serene.

June 6, 1793.

J. W.

POSTSCRIPT.

IN printing a second edition of this letter, it may not be useless to enquire, how far the events which have happened since its first publication correspond to the representations, or illustrate the reasonings, it contains.

Your warmest and most injudicious partizans, Mr. **Pitt**, will not deny that the bankrupt state of the continental powers, our allies, becomes every day more evident.—Englishmen have had a melancholy proof of the nature of the connections they have formed, not merely in the subsidies to Hanover, or to that flower of chivalry the Prince of Hesse (who sells the lives of his subjects at the rate of thirty banco crowns for each), but in the succours demanded by the Austrians to enable them to keep the field; in the ruin of the commerce as well as the finance of Russia (when the ruble, by the regular operations of its government, is reduced, in foreign exchange, to less than half its value); and in that most unprecedented of all treaties with the King of Sardinia, by which we are to pay him two hundred thousand pounds annually, to keep up his own army, for the defence of his own country!

Though the merchants of this kingdom felt the sad effects of the war first, it was predicted that on the manufacturers it would fall with the most unrelenting ruin. The truth of this is now undeniable:—even the woollen and iron branches of manufacture, which in former wars in a great measure escaped, are now almost in a state of stagnation— He who handled the shuttle for three shillings a day, must now take sixpence, and handle the spear;—and many of the enlightened and virtuous assertors of the constitution at Birmingham, so successful in their skirmishes with heresy

and

and the beafts of the flesh, are now doomed to a harder fer-vice on the frontiers of France, where the " Bubble Reputa-tion" must be " fought," not in the libraries or laboratories, or peaceful habitations of unprotected fcience, but in the hoftile fortrefs, " and in the cannon's mouth."

The reafoning refpecting paper-money is alfo con-firmed—So far from this being the caufe of our commercial diftreffes, it is now found, under proper regulations, to be the beft alleviation for them that the times admit ; and a Bank is propofed at Glafgow, and one has been eftablifhed at Liverpool, for this exprefs purpofe.

What was obferved on the fubject of the fuppofed plots and confpiracies, which have fo fatally bewildered the un-derftandings of men, feems alfo to be ftrengthened by the progrefs of events.—The trial of Mr. Froft, from which fo much was expected, is now before the public, and the tender-nefs of the recorder of Leicefter has funk deep into the pub-lic mind.—The zeal and activity of government have infti-tuted various profecutions, and leave no reafon to fuppofe, that, through miftaken lenity, treafon or fedition have been fpared. As yet, however, the fhadow of a confpiracy has not been difcovered——If there be men, Mr. Pitt, lurking in the bofom of their country, who have plotted with France for the deftruction of our conftitution, let their guilty blood ftream on the fcaffold ; the minifter, who would fpare them, is himfelf a traitor—but let not the friends of their king and country, who oppofe your prefent meafures, be involved in fo foul a charge, " to fright the ifle from its propriety," and to involve Us ftill deeper in this ruinous war.

With regard to thofe men who have perfuaded them-felves, that the fafety of England depends on her perfifting in the invafion of France, till monarchy fhall be forced on that kingdom by the allied arms ; the occurrences of the laft two months on the continent may fhake their confidence, and

difpofe

difpofe them to regard, with more attention and alarm, our fituation at home—The fearful diminution of our exifting revenue, and the increafed expenfes of the war, will require, it is evident, new methods and objects of taxation :—thefe our wounded commerce and our diminifhed confumption cannot poffibly fupport; and the neceffity of increafing the land tax is already incurred. But if the war continues, eight fhillings in the pound will do little towards the fupport of the public expenditure, which, even on the peace eftablifhment (if poor-rates be included), already exceeds the grofs amount of all the landlords' rents in England :—a tax on the funds, of which the Dutch have long ago fet us the example, may therefore be expected, and may at laft roufe the monied men from that blind and felfifh acquiefcence in the meafures of every adminiftration, which has been the chief fupport of our war-politics.—A friend, Sir, to the family on the throne, to our limited monarchy, and our conftitution of three eftates—a friend, above all, to the interefts of my country, and the happinefs of the human race, I deprecate the continuance of this dreadful war—My reafons are now before you and the public—However ineffectual my humble exertions may be to ward off the impending calamities, I fhall ftill have the fatisfaction of having performed my duty, and can appeal to the Searcher of Hearts for the purity of my views.

God of peace and love, look down in mercy on thy erring creatures! and bid hatred, madnefs, and murder ceafe !

July 25, 1793.

J. W.

www.ingramcontent.com/pod-product-compliance
Lightning Source LLC
Chambersburg PA
CBHW021526270326
41930CB00008B/1121